"David Avrin is a b[...] the real truth on what your marketing needs to win! If this book were a Western, David would be the sheriff who challenges bad marketing to a showdown!!!"

—Jeffrey Hayzlett, primetime TV and podcast host, Chairman C-Suite Network

"Perhaps the highest compliment one can pay a thought-leader is to simply say that they 'get it.' These words tell you everything you need to know and should act as a not-so-subtle suggestion that you should listen closely to what the thought-leader has to say. David Avrin gets it, and when you read his book, you will too. If you don't, read it twice. I did."

—Bruce Turkel, CEO, Turkel Brands, and author, *Building Brand Value*

Visibility
Marketing

The No-Holds-Barred Truth
About What It Takes to
**Grab Attention,
Build Your Brand,**
and **Win New Business**

DAVID AVRIN

Foreword by Jeffrey Gitomer

CAREER
PRESS

Wayne, NJ

VISIBILITY MARKETING
EDITED BY ROGER SHEETY
TYPESET BY PERFECTYPE, NASHVILLE, TENN.
Cover design by Howard Grossman/12E Design
People image by tai11/shutterstock
Printed in the U.S.A.

To order this title, please call toll-free 1-800-CAREER-1 (NJ and Canada: 201-848-0310) to order using VISA or MasterCard, or for further information on books from Career Press.

CAREER PRESS

The Career Press, Inc.
12 Parish Drive
Wayne, NJ 07470
www.careerpress.com

Library of Congress Cataloging-in-Publication Data

CIP Data Available Upon Request.

For my Dad—an actual rocket scientist
who never really understood marketing,
or what I actually did for a living,
but was always proud of me anyway.

ACKNOWLEDGMENTS

Writing a business book is no simple task, especially when it is not your first. The lessons shared are often a reflection of second generation learning, as much of the existing stockpile of wisdom was shared in the first book. This book went deeper and came from profound lessons gleaned from my life on the road working with audiences and clients.

My first acknowledgment is to the hundreds of companies and organizations, thousands of leaders, and tens of thousands of business audience members across the U.S. and in over 20 countries around the world who have looked to me for wisdom and a measure of entertainment. I guarantee that I have learned as much from your willingness to be vulnerable and share your marketplace challenges, as you have from me.

I owe a great deal to the company leaders in the more than 150 Vistage CEO roundtable groups I have presented for around the world. We go into a room together and close the door. You take off your mask, share your biggest competitive issues and business challenges, and we solve them together. With the vast array of industries represented in the Vistage world, I feel as if I earn a new MBA degree every year.

A big thanks to my literary agent Jill Marsal for your wisdom, guidance, and encouragement. You certainly know your stuff! And to Michael Pye, Lauren Manoy, Roger Sheety, and the entire team at Career Press for your enthusiasm about this book.

To my friends and colleagues: Alan Stevens and Sam Richter for your feedback and suggestions on earlier drafts of this book. Your brilliant insights have made this a much better book!

Thanks to the amazing, irreverent, and brilliant Jeffrey Gitomer for writing the Foreword to this book and for busting my ass to be bold and say what needs to be said. Once again, the book is better because of your wisdom and "encouragement."

A great deal of credit for my business success goes to my Business Manager and "Dave Wrangler" at Visibility International, Tiffany Lauer. You are brilliant, loyal, articulate, efficient, effective, and a pit-bull marketer. Our clients love working with you and it's easy to see why. Thank you!

To my recently-passed father, the brilliant rocket scientist Philip Avrin, who never got to see the end of this project, but was and is the greatest inspiration in my life. Your steadfast work to provide for your family, the no-holds-barred love and affection you showed, and your courage until the end will inspire me for the rest of my days. I miss you and I know that you are proud of me.

To my wonderful children, Sierra, Sydney, and Spencer, who are rapidly transitioning into young adults, my work is for you. I work to not only provide for you, but to model how boldly impacting others' lives can bring great rewards. May you contribute to this world and make a positive impact on those you encounter, as well.

And finally to my sweetheart, Laurel. Your love, kindness, and support gives me fuel to do what I do. Your encouragement and perspective helps me to see what's possible. I'm so grateful you came into my life.

CONTENTS

FOREWORD

Visibility: You Have to See It to Believe It

Whenever you read about something or get a message about something, either by e-mail or socially, there's an ounce of skepticism that goes with it.

"I have to see it to believe it." That's what you say to yourself.

One of the most integral, yet overlooked, parts of marketing is the *big picture* visibility of the brand being touted. And, fortunately, visibility in today's world takes on many faces.

Even more fortunately, David Avrin has identified them and delineated them in a way that you can understand, agree with, and put into action: actions that will make your brand or product talked about and visible; actions that will make the written elements about your brand or product visible in a new way; and actions that will make your brand or product visible by being written about, talked about, perceived as different, perceived as valuable and, of course, buyable.

The importance of this book cannot simply be written about. When I agreed to write the foreword for *Visibility Marketing* (and I write very few), I realized that this was a book that was an imperative, not simply a lesson or a "how to" book.

Visibility is the new black. And you don't have to take my word for it. Look at YouTube and the many lesser brands that promote video as a way of communicating. Video is another word for visibility.

Of course, video is not the only way to be visible, but keep in mind that they don't call it "TextTube" for a reason. It is for that very same reason that the visibility element of a testimonial "letter" is as passé as a fax machine or a Blackberry.

Visibility has morphed during the last two decades: the newspaper want-ad is now Craigslist and the *Yellow Pages* is now Google (the taxi is now Uber, but that should be for David's next book called: *Standing Still and Watching Your Competition Bury You!*).

Do you want some hints about visibility?

- **○** Posting is the new visibility.
- **○** Social selling is the new visibility.

- E-mail is the new visibility.
- Tweeting is the new visibility.
- Blogging is the new visibility.
- LinkedIn is the new visibility.
- Instagram is the new visibility (just an FYI: Microsoft Word still thinks Instagram is a misspelled word).
- Facebook is the new visibility.
- And, of course, face-to-face is the gold standard in visibility.

Seriously, when was the last time you received an actual letter in the mail and called one of your colleagues over, yelling, "Hey Bob, come here, you gotta read this letter!"?

But that's the *small* picture of visibility.

The *big* picture of visibility is more fundamental and foundational to your product, service, or brand's market impact:

- It's word selection in everything you write.
- It's differentiation *from* your competition.
- It's perceived value by the customer.
- It's not how great you are; it's how the customer wins.
- It's not about being a good choice; it's about being the best choice.

- ❍ It's not being "one of," it's being the "only one."
- ❍ It's not we-we, it's you-you.

Value-driven visibility takes time. And the customer must perceive it beyond your bragging. Testimonials create more visibility (YouTube) than brochures (shredder).

A word of caution: being visibly price competitive is only good if you want to be profit deprived.

The visibility process must be studied, planned, and implemented so it can be shared to exponentially build positive marketplace awareness (without a fight from someone with nine Twitter followers).

My visibility *aha* moments will be your *aha* moments as well.

When David and I talked about this book and the message he was trying to convey, he simply said:

> Jeffrey, too many people think that it all comes down to quality. No!! Quality is merely the entry fee that allows you to play in the sandbox.
>
> Today *everyone* is good. If they weren't, they wouldn't survive for long. Don't tell us why you are a good choice, but prove to us that you are a better choice than the others who are good.

Why then do so many still believe that quality is the great differentiator? "At the end of the day, it's really about quality," the hapless leader will offer, totally missing the shift that has occurred under their very watch.

No! At the *beginning* of the day it's about quality! Today, being really, really good at what you do gives you permission to be in business. At the *end* of the day it's about "competitive advantage." It's not what you do well. It's what you do better than everyone else.

Got it!

And *Visibility Marketing* will make the beginning of *the* day, the beginning of *your* day, the same way it made mine. Today is that day. Read on.

Jeffrey Gitomer

Author of *The Little Red Book of Selling*

AUTHOR'S NOTE
PSST. DON'T SKIP THIS!

Although the word "marketing" is front and center in the title, this is first and foremost a business book for business owners, organizational leaders and their teams, sales professionals, and anyone responsible for building companies and bringing products and services to the marketplace.

If you picked up this book looking for "100 Ways to Promote Your Business," you won't find it here. If you were interested in an academic analysis of buying trends and behaviors, you are out of luck. This book is intentionally more strategic than tactical, although tactics are discussed. This book is about a profound shift in how we buy and how you sell. It is as much a cautionary tome as it is a strategic roadmap for success.

Put more simply, this book is more anecdotal than academic, more conversational than conventional, more personal than pragmatic, more observational than empirical, and it is written for the ear as much as it is for the page.

Despite what you might have been taught in school, feel free to write all over this book. Highlight passages, dog-ear the pages, write in the margins, and photocopy the exercises and pass them out to your team.

Marketing is not a passive endeavor. It can get messy at times. Go grab yourself a cup of coffee, roll up your sleeves, and let's get to work.

David Avrin, CSP

The Visibility Coach

CHAPTER 1

Nice Work. Now Get Over Yourself!

"Hey Dad," my then 11-year-old son Spencer calls out to me from his perch on the couch across the family room. Friends and family had converged at my home in the South Denver suburb of Castle Rock, Colorado to watch the Super Bowl. "I was just wondering," Spencer says, "if they can make such great commercials for the Super Bowl, why don't they just make great commercials during the rest of the year?"

This unexpected, but insightful, question caught me off guard. "Yeah, marketing genius," my brother chides me from across the room, "answer that one!"

After a brief pause to carefully consider my response, I began:

"Buddy," I say to my son, "the truth is that people in businesses can create really great, funny, cool, interesting, or memorable marketing anytime they decide to and are willing to work hard at it. It just seems more important for them to work harder to be creative when the commercials cost a lot more money—like during the Super Bowl. The rest of the year, quite honestly, they are just being lazy. They don't take the time or push themselves to come up with really great ideas. Worse yet, companies just say 'yes' to bad or boring commercials and campaigns that ad agencies and marketing firms make for them, because they trust the 'experts'—who are just being lazy."

"Is that what you do when you go work with clients or give speeches, Dad?" he asks, "tell people to not be lazy?"

"Sometimes," I say, smiling. "A lot of business owners don't really know any better. So, I show them why what they are doing and saying isn't working very well. I teach them ways to be creative all year long, and I push them to not accept anything that isn't great. And I also make them laugh," I add, "so they will listen to me."

"You're kind of like their marketing coach."

"Yes, Spencer. That's exactly what I am."

Business marketing is like competitive sports in so many ways. There are teammates, opponents, fans, strategy, tactics, preparation, and execution. Make no mistake; there are also winners and losers as the "game" is being played out in a very public forum. Oh, and the score is always being kept. Always.

The most significant difference between business and sports, however, is that the outcome of the business marketing game determines who actually survives as an entity to play again and who does not. It's not merely the fans that walk away disappointed, with the next game scheduled for the following week. No, it's families that lose homes, children who miss out on college options, relationships that are strained, and entrepreneurs who are robbed of their livelihood and their dreams along with it. In business, there is so much more at stake.

There is a systemic and wide-reaching dynamic in today's world of business marketing: most of it sucks. Okay, maybe that's not the most technical or articulate way of putting it, but it is essentially true. Despite the emergence of some powerful new tactics made possible by the pervasive reach of the Web and mobile technology, the basic tenants of business marketing have remained the same for decades. The problem is that most of the approaches of yesteryear are no longer effective. We've become jaded. The hard truth is that the mind-numbing sameness of inadvertent "commodity marketing" rules the day.

Too many in business have failed to recognize the shift that has happened right under their very noses. It's not so much that people have changed; it's that the business landscape has changed—dramatically. For the first time in human history, we have no unmet needs. Every problem has a solution and, too often today, companies find themselves scrambling to create solutions that appear to be looking for a problem. Selection is vast, quality abounds, and international competition in many categories have driven prices down to the point where even the poorest among us has access to services, items, and amenities that were once reserved for the affluent.

The once-effective go-to marketing messages have been diluted to the point of being largely dismissible. The historic marketing claims of superior quality, greater reliability, caring service, passionate, committed people, and the freshest ingredients are falling on deaf ears. Yet the claims persist. I say: *lazy!*

You can do better, much better! Owners, entrepreneurs, marketing and sales professionals, and other stakeholders need a harsh wake-up call. They need to be grabbed by the shoulders, smacked on the helmet, and told to stop settling for mediocre messages and marketing that merely inform and take up time and space, but don't differentiate. Today, effective marketing is not about competence, it's about creating and communicating competitive advantage.

The landscape is littered with the corpses of great products and strong companies which died from lazy marketing. There is so much bad marketing that a telecast to "honor" the worst of the worst would go on for weeks. This book aims to stem the tide. For those that heed the call, the rewards can be great! For those that don't, "Sorry, what was your name again?"

So, what is visibility marketing? In days gone by, visibility was about being seen where you are. You wanted the biggest neon sign or the brightest paint on your building. You hired a kid to hold a sandwich board or dress as a company mascot and wave at passing cars. You held contests and drawings to get people on-site by reminding them that "you must be present to win." If there was an opportunity to buy beyond the confines of your location, it was through a catalogue you printed and mailed out. (Receiving the Sears Christmas *Wish Book* was a highlight of my years as a kid!)

Today, visibility marketing is about being visible where your prospective customers and clients are. It's every way they can see you, engage with you, hear about you, and access you. It's about engaging them where they work, where they shop, play, eat, and gather. Visibility marketing is about your wisdom or expertise front and center on their smartphones. It's about your video promotion or location tours streaming on their laptops, and your thoughts, wisdom, or playful banter engaging them on social media. It's about connecting your brand with them at the events they attend, reality shows they watch, and blogs they read. Visibility marketing is about connecting what you offer with the life they live—not on the periphery, not where you are, but integrated into how they spend their days.

Visibility marketing is also about the real impact you make, the customers you thrill, and the breadcrumbs you leave behind. And although it's becoming trite to repeat the well-worn adage that "marketing is not a department," it's truer today than ever before. Every interaction with a client is an opportunity to either create a raving brand ambassador or fuel an online detractor. Word-of-mouth has always been an important element in building a strong brand, but today those personal impressions have a global audience. Before making a significant purchase, we look to others—online and otherwise—to gauge marketplace impressions before moving forward. How good you are, and how consistently good you are, matters—a lot!

Traditional "guest-relations" philosophy asserted something along the lines of: the average person with a positive experience with a business will tell two or three people, whereas a person with a negative experience will tell 10. Today, both positive and negative experiences are shared with millions or even billions! And although those who are the most frustrated are the most diligent online sharers, the enthusiastic advocates are your best marketing assets.

The point is that you are already visible! The only two questions are: What are people seeing, hearing, and learning about you? And how many people are you reaching?

This new dynamic is not over the horizon, it is already here and influencing everything in our business and our lives. Visibility marketing is about how to recognize this pervasive dynamic and maximize the opportunities that it provides.

It's not merely about using the new tools, vehicles, and venues, it's about doing it better than everyone else—and many others are doing it well!

This book is about how applying traditional promotional thinking to the new reality wastes dollars, loses customers, and ruins businesses. Most simply don't get it. You will.

Like no other time in human history, choices abound. From a staggering array of breakfast cereals, smartphones and tablets, disposable wipes, fast-casual restaurants, and ultra HD televisions, to gluten-free items, financial planners, all-season tires, and treatments for erectile dysfunction, we have a staggering number of choices. We can buy in-person, on our computers and smartphones, over the phone, and even through our television. We can have our items mailed, shipped, downloaded, couriered, or even delivered by drone. Convenience and selection rule the day.

There was a time when touting our commitment to our employees, caring for our customers, passion about our products, outstanding customer service, integrity, honesty, commitment, and superior quality carried weight. In days gone by, the varying levels of quality and spotty service delivery brought with it widespread distrust and a "buyer beware" mentality. Those days are over.

Today, everyone is good and many are truly outstanding. You don't agree? Wake up!

I still hear company leaders say: "At the end of the day, it's really about quality." Wrong! At the beginning of the day, it's about quality. Producing and providing high-quality products and services are merely the cost of entry into today's marketplace. Everybody is good, so you'd better be good as well. At the end of the day, it's about competitive advantage. Winning the business is about adding value. It's about nuance. It's about not merely being marginally better, but being a *clearly* better choice. It's about preferability, deeper connection, astonishing ease of doing business, hyper-convenience, remarkable innovation, tangibly superior quality, and of course, visibility.

As I travel the world speaking and working with entrepreneurs, CEOs, sales and leadership teams, and their organizations, one of the most deeply ingrained beliefs that they share is that they are great and most of their competitors are simply not as good. There is a pervasive belief that their competitors consistently underperform and are somehow fooling their customers and prospects. "The difference with us," leaders will say with a measure of indignation, "is that we actually do what we say we will do!"

Really? Do you honestly believe that? How on God's green Earth are your competitors still in business with all of their supposed "not doing what they say they will do"? Ridiculous!

Seriously people, it's time for a reality check. Your competitors are good—really good. Do you know why people do business with your competitors? They do so because they want to, because they like them, and because they chose them (instead of choosing you!). You had better figure out why if you want to survive and grow.

As much as you would like to believe otherwise, most of your competitors are not only good at what they do, but they are actually very nice people. If you weren't in competition, you'd probably be friends with them. They work hard, listen to their customers, care about quality, work to thrill their clients, treat them well, and live up to their promises. Every day, your competitors are providing livelihoods for their employees, forging meaningful relationships with their customers, working long hours, and getting better all the time. And you? To be fair, you might be doing much of the same, but face it—you are just another in a long list of choices for your prospective customers.

It has often been said that the first step to overcoming a problem is to admit that you have one.

The problem is that you are likely a little overly enamored with yourself. Sorry, if you find that insulting. This is not about believing in yourself and following your dreams. I'm referring to your business. You are likely very good at what you do, but you're not *that* good. You haven't created the cure for cancer that tastes like chocolate, or solved the cold-fusion conundrum. If you were *that* good, you wouldn't need to market your talents, company, products, or services. To be fair, none of us are that good. You need to market. And to market effectively, you need to understand both your customers and your competitors.

There are three indisputable trends that have contributed to the diminishing effectiveness of the "quality, service, integrity, caring, and people" marketing claims:

First, the "quality process improvement" (CQI, TQM, Six Sigma, Kaizen, and so on) movement through the past 30 years has actually been remarkably effective, raising the bar for everyone. Quite simply, everyone has gotten much better. Big business learned important lessons and raised their game. Small businesses have learned from big business and everyone has gotten better.

There are no shortages of resources helping business owners improve their leadership, processes, logistics, finances, and operations. Business speakers (my colleagues) teach and inspire audiences, business coaches develop leaders, articles inform, videos demonstrate, and business books—good business books—challenge conventional wisdom. You'd be foolish not to avail yourself of this pervasive wisdom to improve your business and shorten your learning curve. Millions have expanded their knowledge, skill-sets, and perspective on how to build and run effective, successful businesses. The result is a rising tide that has raised all ships and created a more competitive marketplace and, along with it, an often daunting barrier to entry. Once again, quality abounds.

Secondly, the recent profound downturn in the economy has weeded out the lesser players and spurred significant consolidation. What happened to those companies which, coming out of very challenging economic times, were not strategic, didn't make hard, painful cuts streamlining their operation, didn't have a sounding board like a CEO peer-advisory group or professional coach, and didn't form synergistic partnerships and strategic alliances? Oh yeah, they didn't survive, or they were reduced to such an extent that they are no longer meaningful competitors. The ones that did survive are stronger, smarter, and leaner.

Finally, in this instantaneous-feedback, tech-in-your-pocket access to everything, and on-demand Internet age, the market's tolerance for underperformance has essentially shrunk to zero. Everyone is good, because if they weren't, people would know—quickly. In yesteryear, a bad movie could survive for weeks in theaters. Today, moviegoers are warned immediately of bad releases by both legitimate critics and the public at large. A poor interaction with a restaurant worker, an airline ticket agent, or even the police can be uploaded and shared with millions of people in seconds. You have to be good, because if you weren't, we would know. Everything is visible: the good, bad, and very ugly.

Today, everyone in business is good, as the bad ones are quickly "outed" to the masses. It doesn't mean that stragglers don't exist, as there will always be stragglers that get away with some measure of underperformance. I'm saying that those companies aren't really your competitors, or won't be for very long. Their poor online reviews, one-star ratings, and poor word-of-mouth will cause others to disregard them quickly. If they are surviving merely because they are far cheaper, then you don't want their customers anyway.

Here's the difficult truth: your business could disappear from the face of the Earth today, and aside from some very sad family members and employees, the marketplace would barely miss you. I'm not suggesting that you aren't doing great work and I'm sure your customers really like you. It's that if you went out of business, your competitors would gladly step in and absorb your previous customers and even your employees. In fact, tens of thousands of businesses fail every year, and we seem to be getting along just fine without them.

Of course, there have always been sub-par or shady operations and questionable professional practices. In the past, these "posers" could find a way to fly under the radar and still eke out a reasonable living. Those days are long gone. There may be sporadic examples of underperformance by competitors, but I promise you it is the exception rather than the rule. They fix problems, just as you do. They respond to complaints and work to make things right.

The reality is that your competitors are not just very good; in some tangible ways, some are better than you!

With the prevalence of social media and instantaneous customer service feedback and ratings from the likes of Yelp, TripAdvisor, and more, poor experiences become public grist very quickly—often instantaneously! Poor service is no longer private. Bad treatment becomes Internet fodder within minutes, and this dynamic is not lost on corporations. Companies hire teams to monitor social media discussions and comments 24/7 to quickly respond to and address customer dissatisfaction.

One has to merely add the hashtag #UnitedAirlines to a Twitter or Facebook rant and a response from the company is only seconds away. It's not simply because they are "customer-focused," or "customer-centric." No. They got burned for a delayed response (search: "United Breaks Guitars") and they are not going to be caught flat-footed again.

With my keynote speaking, I travel extensively throughout the world and I prefer to rent my cars from Enterprise. They provide consistently great customer service (and they gladly take my debit card). Whenever I return my car to Enterprise at the end of my trip, I am greeted by a predictably efficient worker with a smiling face.

"Welcome back, Mr. Avrin," the rep says, as they walk around the car checking for damage. "How was the [insert car model here]?"

"Fine, thank you," I respond, gathering my luggage from the trunk of the car.

"Did you have a chance to fill it up?" they inquire.

"Nope. Go ahead and charge me," I say, as always.

And then, as they tear off the receipt from the hand-held printer, the representative looks up and asks me the same question every time: "Is there anything we could have done to make this a more outstanding experience for you?"

What they are really saying to me is: "Please, please don't go online to TripAdvisor and trash us for something we could have fixed today! If there is anything—anything at all—that you didn't like, please, please tell me so that I can make it right!!"

Bad experience may be short lived, but the online rant is immortal. It's a cynical view to be sure, but I remind my three kids (now in their teens and 20s) often about the dangers of poorly considered social media posts. I ask them: "Do you know the difference between love and the Internet? Yep. The Internet is forever . . . and ever!"

Just as my cynical admonition to my children illustrates, we need to do everything we can to share and promote only that which makes us look attractive and preferable to our customers and prospects, and work hard to prevent the negative items from forever tarnishing our reputation. First and foremost, we have to correct problems so the ammunition doesn't exist to be shared. Every client or customer has the potential of leaving dissatisfied. It's your job to do everything in your power to prevent that from happening.

This universal "raising-of-the-bar" has created a marketplace replete with quality, talent, reasonable prices, and good service. In short, commodity abounds.

Google the phrase "Why businesses fail" and the first several pages are filled with links leading to list after list, article after article, pointing to a dearth of leadership, culture, teamwork, collaboration, innovation, vision, and more. Although those may be contributing factors to why companies fail to grow, the primary reason that businesses fail to survive is that they don't have enough customers and sales. They don't have enough customers and sales because they do a poor job of differentiating themselves from strong competitors and gaining visibility.

Despite what you may hear from politicians and others about the "explosion" of business start-ups, the numbers of new businesses are misleading because the majority of them ultimately fail. That's like telling your kids there is plenty of food in the refrigerator, even though most of it is spoiled and inedible.

The marketplace has changed, and good, hard-working people are getting crushed. The business failure rate today is staggering and growing each year. In fact, more small businesses have failed in the last five years than even existed in 1960. What's the number one reason? Not enough customers. Shocker!

Here's the truth, the hard truth: being really, really good at what you do is no longer a differentiator. Today, it is nothing more than the entry fee. If you don't have great quality, strong customer service, keep promises, and deliver what your customers want, then you will not survive. Today, we want to do more than merely survive and compete. We want to win! The "new normal" is a marketplace populated by very good companies who are great at what they do. Dismiss them at your own peril.

You've heard it before: "In sales, there is no prize for second place." You get the gig, or you don't. You make the sale, or you don't. Unlike your 10-year-old son or daughter, business doesn't hand out "participation ribbons" or trophies for merely being on the team. In sales, second place is the first loser. The winner eats. The loser doesn't.

So, how can you be known, not just as a good choice, but as the best choice for . . . something?

I'm a big believer that you have to be known as the best choice for one thing; or one problem; or one need; or one industry; or one geographic area. I'm not suggesting that you can't offer a broad spectrum of products and services. I'm simply saying that you have to "own" something in the minds of your prospects. You have to win on something. And it can be anything, but it has to be something. It can be a proprietary technology, an outrageous persona, prolific distribution or physical locations, an iconic product, celebrity endorser, signature product, famous client, recognizable design, and even lowest price—though that's not really a game that you want to play.

Here's another way to look at it: *To what question are you the answer?* What question would elicit your name as not just a good choice, but the *best* choice?

For example, if I wanted to purchase a very safe car, you might suggest a Volvo. Volvo owns *safety* in your mind. Okay, don't challenge me with assertions of new safety leaders like Toyota, Honda, or even Tesla. Volvo owns the words "safe car" in your mind. With the safety innovations pioneered by Volvo in the late 1960s and early 1970s, Volvo earned its "mind share" as the safety innovator. And despite the fact that all of those safety innovations have been replicated or even surpassed in recent years, Volvo still owns that spot in the public consciousness. Whether they still want it or not, Volvo has the image of the quintessential, upper middle class, white, male, conservative, suburban, Connecticut, dad-car.

If I were to ask: What department store has the best customer service? You will, of course, respond: Nordstrom. What about online retail customer service? You might say: Zappos, Amazon, or GoDaddy.

Clearly, these top-of-mind associations did not come about merely by proclamation and intention. They earned it! The structure in their organizations supports the vision for what they aspired to become in your mind. They've created policies, procedures, and behaviors that manifested in an alignment between their claims and your experience. Through innovation, consistent delivery, empowered employees, and other specific behaviors, over time they've became known for what they wanted to be known for.

So, the question for you is: What category can you own in the mind of your prospects? I'm not referring to market share. This is about "mind share." Mind share comes before market share. Before you are open to buying a product, hiring a professional, or contracting for a service, you have to know what it is. You have to be familiar with it, understand its benefits, and trust in its promise. Mind share is earned over time with strong messaging, repeated exposure, and consistently positive experiences.

There has been a profound shift in the marketplace during the past 25 years. I'm not referring to the shift from analogue to digital, but the profound shift from selling to buying. In yesteryear, it was the salesperson that ruled the interaction and drove the transaction. We needed salespeople to educate us on products and services, features, and benefits. We only knew what we knew, and the little that we did know, we learned from advertisements or word-of-mouth. The salesperson knew more. We needed them to help us avoid making a bad decision.

In yesteryear, we would go to an appliance store and rely on the salesperson to educate us about the newest refrigerator or washer and dryer. If we wanted to compare models, we would drive to another store and talk to their salesperson.

We would walk into a car dealership and walk around the car. Then we would get inside and play with the knobs, pretending we were driving it. Then we would motion the salesperson over, who has been hovering nearby and ask: "So, tell us about this car." We don't do that anymore. Today, when we walk into a dealership we likely know everything about that car. We've done side-by-side comparisons online. We know the features and probably even know what the dealer paid for that car.

In the not-so-distant past, we would visit the doctor, explain our symptoms, and ask: "What is wrong with me?" Today, we go into the doctor's office and say: "Here is what is wrong with me. This is the medication I want . . ." We've self-diagnosed! We have the information at our fingertips and we have taken control of the transaction.

I'm not suggesting that there is no longer a role for the salesperson. It's that the role has shifted. Your job is no longer to merely provide education about features and benefits—we already know those. Your job is to tell us, show us, and clearly demonstrate why your product is a better choice than all the other good options available to us.

The business world has become one gigantic grocery store. We walk the aisles selecting what we want to buy, with no assistance from a salesperson. Nobody sells us anything at a grocery store. We buy things. In fact, there is only one question you are likely to be asked at a grocery store: "Paper or plastic?"

When we can simply browse and select what we want to buy, becoming the best or obvious choice in a vast sea of choices becomes all the more imperative. In your category, if you've established your quality and competitive pricing, you've merely paid the entry fee. You need to discover and promote the reason that you are the best choice in your category.

So, here is the most important question posed in this book: What makes you a clearly better choice than all the other good choices in the marketplace?

Okay, please don't bore me (or your prospects) with outdated and meaningless responses such as: "Our people make the difference." "We use only the freshest ingredients." "Our customers come first." Or, how about this one: "We really listen to our clients and we tailor our solutions to meet their individual needs." Blech!

Whether it was you or someone else who founded your company, you've likely spent years, if not decades, building your reputation, gaining experience, and fostering relationships. You may have spent tens of thousands—or perhaps even millions—of dollars building infrastructure, logistical processes, facilities, and capacity. But chances are you've only spent minutes crafting the words you use to describe what you do. If you have an outside marketing firm or advertising agency, maybe you've spent an hour or two. Because despite what your marketing or ad agency may tell you, that's how long it takes to write the copy for your website or brochure—about an hour.

What if you did a deeper dive to truly evaluate the words you use to promote yourself, or your products and services? What if you treated yourself like a client and gave yourself your undivided attention to discover, uncover, craft, create, and communicate legitimate competitive advantage? What if you decided to block a day off your calendar, grab your team, pile into the conference room, turn off your cell phones, order take-out, set up a few flip charts, roll up your sleeves, and start asking some hard questions about why your prospects should choose you? What might you discover about yourself?

WTF is a popular (though crude) texting shortcut that has become part of the broader Millennial lexicon, perhaps because it so effectively sums up the exasperation that so many people feel in response to outrageous words or actions, and because we want to say it—without actually saying it. (And it's because teenagers think they're using clever codes so we don't know what they're really saying. But we do.)

A more appropriate variation for this book is WTV or "What's the visibility?" It's a question you should ask yourself every time you consider developing or offering a new product, service, policy, marketing idea, website enhancement, or more. Ask yourself: "WTV? How will that make us more visible?" Or how about ROV? What's the "Return on visibility?" How will that product, promotion, event, or article make people understand what makes us a better choice? How will it make us more attractive, accessible, affordable, buzzworthy, memorable and, of course, *visible*?

By the same token, every time you are approached by a salesperson offering to put your ad on the back of the bathroom stall in some popular restaurant or your flyer on the doors of homes in an adjacent neighborhood, ask WTV? Don't just ask yourself, "Will this increase my visibility?" but also, "How will it do so in a way that is aligned with who I want to be in the marketplace and how I want to be known and remembered?"

Beyond the admittedly overly simplistic way of using the abbreviated question to gauge the effectiveness of potential initiatives, it is also an important self-assessment exercise before embarking on the lessons of this book. Take a step back and assess all of your current marketing efforts by asking the same simple question: WTV?

Exercise: WTV? Self-Assessment Test

Take out a piece of paper and divide into four columns. At the top, label each vertical column starting left to right: Media/Venue, Your Company Name, Your Nearest Competitor, and Your Next Nearest Competitor. (Of course, put your name and the actual names of your competitors.)

Down the left column, list:

LinkedIn

Facebook

Twitter

Pinterest

Instagram

Google (search ranking)

YouTube (search rankings)

Blogs

External Signage (your physical location)

Article Placement

News Appearances

Online Reviews (Yelp, TripAdvisor, etc.)

Print Advertisements

Sponsorships

Local Chambers-of-Commerce

Community Service

And other places where you promote (and any other place where prospects might see and hear you)

On a scale of 1–10, with 10 being the most visible you can be, rate yourself on your current level of visibility for each of the "media/venues." Then do the same for your competitors. Remember, you need to do this from the perspective of a prospective customer. How much do they know about you if they weren't already doing business with you?

Now, ask someone else who knows you, but doesn't work for you, or who isn't a customer, to fill it out as well—without seeing your answers.

Once completed, sit with your team (if you have one) and rank the different items in the first column as to which ways to be visible are the most important for your business. Where do your prospects get their information? Where do they shop? Where do they connect with friends and other influencers? Rank the items with "1" being the most important, "2" as next important, and so on.

Finally, discuss with your team what can be done to bolster your "WTV" number for each one and assign a responsibility. Jot notes next to each one capturing all the ideas. This book will give many more ideas to bolster your initial notes, but this is an important initial assessment.

The most successful companies, brands, and people have a high degree of both popularity and visibility. In other words, they are both well-known and well-liked. Those in business who fail to reach their full potential have some level of deficiency in one of the two areas.

Keep in mind that your current status is often fluid with companies, products, and people falling in and out of favor with their core audience. Today's hot product can be yesterday's fad and today's unknown political candidate can quickly rise through the ranks—and fall just as quickly.

The key is to know where you are and where you aspire to be, so that you can plot a course to get there. Take a few steps back and look at your business objectively.

_____

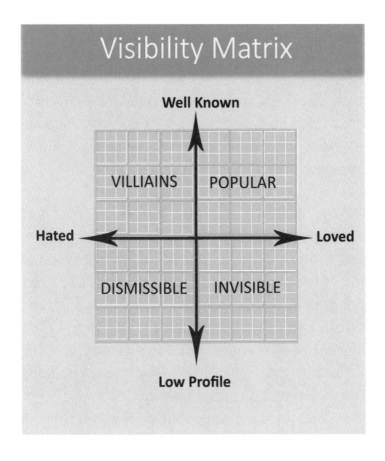

Looking at the graph, give yourself an honest assessment of both your visibility and likability. Keep in mind that your assessment needs to be from the perspective of a prospective customer or client. I know that your current customers like you; that's why they buy from you. I'm trying to help you grow your business! Who should be doing business with you, but is not yet doing so?

Using the Matrix, plot where you are today and then where you would like to be in one year, three years, and so on. Draw a line from where you are to where you want to be. Then, using a different color, plot your nearest competitors and their likely trajectory.

The Lower Left (LL) section means both unknown and disliked. At the farthest extreme, it might be a business who you don't ever want to have to do business with, like a loan shark or a bail bonds man. But as you move around the quadrant, things can change dramatically. Perhaps a new owner to a local shop is battling previous poor performance and desires to move to the Lower Right (LR) before inching their way up.

You can also be very well known, but tremendously disliked. Think Martin Shkreli, the hedge fund millionaire whose pharmaceutical company bought a life-saving drug and raised the price by 5,000 percent. Think, also, about Bill Cosby. 'Nuff said. But for some in the UL (Upper Left) Villains quadrant, redemption is possible. British Petroleum suffered catastrophic damage to their reputation when oil poured into the Gulf Mexico after an oil rig explosion. But through significant investment in cleanup, community investment, and smart, consistent messaging, they have regained much good will. BP Moved from UL to cross the line into UR (Upper Right).

The popular fresh Mexican chain, Chipotle enjoyed years of Upper Right placement, with a focus on positive messaging, fresh, locally-sourced food, natural ingredients, and a casual vibe. Unfortunately, along with the rejection of corporate food sources came a lapse in quality control and a rash of food-borne illnesses in late 2015. They quickly moved to UL and it might take years to recover from this damage. To their credit, Chipotle took immediate action and provided a very transparent revamp of their quality control process, but the damage was done. Crisis management is vitally important, but the best strategy is to address problems before they ever emerge. Your reputation is tenuous at best. Protect it.

Is this marketing? Of course it is! Everything is marketing, including everything you say about yourself and everything that others say about you. If we can envision and execute the experience, then we can have a great influence on the experience our customers receive and how they talk about us to others. We can build a billion dollar brand, but if one of your vendors passes along a pathogen that makes your customers sick, you are sending a message you hadn't planned for.

The questions are: Where are you on the Matrix today? Where can you realistically move to and what is it going to take to get you there? Keep in mind that your placement and that of your competitors is never static. It's always fluid! You can move up or down, left or right. The key is to keep within your control as much of the movement as you can.

LL—Dismissible
Trajectory: Journey to Worthy or Descend into Darkness

Tactics:

Introduce to the market

Craft a compelling story

Rapid emergence

Rags to riches

UL—Villains
Trajectory: Road to Redemption or Lost Cause

Tactics:

Change your ways

Reveal truth

Second chance

Reemergence

Comeback kid!

LR—Invisible
Trajectory: Path to Popularity or Relegated to Anonymity
> Tactics:
> Promotion
> Shine a light
> Tell your story
> Highlight differentiators
> Convert prospects
> Create ambassadors

UR—Popular
Trajectory: Bolster Your Brand or Flash-in-the-Pan
> Tactics:
> Stay hungry
> Keep innovating
> Remain visible
> Reinforce message
> Recruit new champions

Now that you have a clearer idea of where you are, it's time to plot a course to get you where you want to go.

CHAPTER 2

Who Do the Voodoo That You Do So Well?

Imagine that you have a floating ball in front of your face. Think of this as your brand today. Walk around it in your mind and pretend you are looking at your business, not just from the customer's perspective, but from an all-knowing, omnipotent, and potential customer. What do you look like to the marketplace? How much money do you make? What is your signature product or service? Who are your high-profile clients or customers? How many times have you "rocked the house" with customers and how many times have you fallen short?

If you are familiar with the concept of leading and lagging indicators, your brand today is a lagging indicator. You are looking in the rearview mirror. Everything that you have done up until today has contributed to where you are. As of today, the amount of money you make is the amount you make. You are as famous as you are and you have just as many loyal customers as you have earned. Today is the baseline from where you are starting this process of charting your course.

So, what do you aspire to? What is next for you and your business? What does success look like for you? It's different for everyone, of course. For some, success means being able to take two months off each year and to travel. For others, success means complete and utter world domination.

When I say "success" I am not referring to operational excellence, logistical efficiency, or great customer service. Those are merely *foundational*; it is the cost of doing business. You had better be good at those things, because your competitors surely are.

To truly excel in today's hyper-competitive categories, you have to master the "foundational" and then focus on the "aspirational." This isn't about what your customers aspire to—it's what *you* aspire to! You have to decide and commit to being better than your competitors and do everything within your power to make it happen! You have to be better at something meaningful, memorable, and tangible and more effectively market your competitive advantage, not merely your talents and core competency.

The good news is that your competitors are likely promoting the same over-used foundational qualities as well. This is where your opportunity lies! Take a step back and explore the things you offer that others don't. What can you claim that others can't? What accepted shortcoming in your industry can you no longer accept, but instead develop and offer a unique solution, alternative delivery, or better deliverable?

Most marketing books focus on tactics to effectively market your business. And though I will certainly address many, my focus is on helping you become more strategic and "marketable." This is not merely about crafting clever language. I promise you that it will be a lot easier to craft great messages when you have discovered or created something remarkable to talk about.

You are likely crafting your marketing messages and creating materials and a website in a vacuum. You simply look at your company, products, services, and value proposition and create persuasive and descriptive verbiage that describes what you do and connects them to your audience. There's nothing inherently wrong with that and I'm not suggesting that you don't try to be very engaging, descriptive, and persuasive. But, what people too often forget is that competitors are targeting the same prospects—often with similar, if not identical claims.

How do you effectively compete against competitors until you are clear with how they are competing against you? You think you are having a one-on-one conversation with prospects. You aren't! You are on a party line and many others are talking with them as well, often with the exact same language. Your prospects only know what they know and if they are hearing essentially the same things from your competitors, then you are losing the battle.

Before charting a path or exploring marketing tactics, we have to be clear about where you really want to go. The real question is: Where would you like to take your business? That is not a rhetorical question. You have to have specific targets in mind so you can chart a path to get there.

Look for a reasonable time in your future and set some achievable, aspirational goals for your business or your personal success within your organization. For example: "We want to be the leading authority in the marketplace for X." "We are going to be the go-to resource for Y," or "the top-of-mind, best choice for Z."

Because when you have clarity of goals and have consensus among your team, then you can begin to align all of your organizational activities to achieve them. Look at your hiring. Are the people you are bringing in or supervising the right people to help you get where you want and effectively deliver both your products and your messages? Are you aligning your training, research and development, processes, new product development, project management, service delivery, customer service and, of course, your marketing messages to achieve that marketplace goal and ownership spot in the minds of your customers and prospects?

To make this stick, you have to make certain that your business structure supports your vision. In other words, can you deliver all that you want to claim? Have you created policies, procedures, products, and a culture to ensure that you are delivering with what you are claiming—consistently?

Nordstrom is renowned for their great customer service, but their reputation did not come about by merely proclaiming their superior service. Everybody claims it. The powers-that-be at Nordstrom likely sat in a room with their team and said: "We are in a highly competitive space, people!

There is Saks Fifth Ave., Neiman Marcus, Bergdorf Goodman, and more. What are we better at?"

The easy answer is just to take care of the customer better than anyone else. But as a claim it is meaningless unless there are policies and procedures that guarantee their people deliver a high level of service on a consistent basis. There have to be specific behaviors that are taught, modeled, encouraged, reinforced, and constantly evaluated. There have to be policies, visible to the customer, that separate Nordstrom from the others in their space who also deliver high-end service.

So, what did Nordstrom do? They empowered their frontline staff to make decisions, even at the risk of profit, to ensure stellar customer satisfaction. They don't need to find a manager to solve problems. They share stories of extraordinary service from their team where they exemplify the service mantra. You know, we all know, that you can take anything back at Nordstrom. That policy takes the risk out of pricey purchases and puts them in a different category in terms of claimed customer service. Translation: they stand behind their claims.

There is a famous story that tells of Nordstrom taking back a year-old set of snow tires, no questions asked. And, of course, the rub of the story is—wait for it—they don't sell tires! Whether this is truthful or merely an urban legend, I don't really care. It fits! The tale takes a known benefit of shopping at Nordstrom and reinforces it by taking it to a ridiculous level. It works because you believe Nordstrom might actually go to ridiculous lengths to make you happy.

However, there is a cost to changes in policy and bolstering your brand by creating new and enhanced value propositions. Nordstrom knows that some will take advantage of the policy. It's inevitable. For Nordstrom, the cost includes taking back a certain amount of prom dresses the day after prom. "It didn't fit?" the clerk inquires with a smile. "I am so sorry. How was prom, by the way? I'm sure you were beautiful!" The cost is minuscule; the reputation reinforcement is priceless.

As I travel extensively speaking throughout the U.S. and around the world, I stay in too many hotel rooms to count. Although I am often spoiled by luxury accommodations in magnificent and exotic locations, I also stay at my fair share of small, chain hotels. One of the most remarkable examples of creating competitive advantage comes from Hampton Inn hotels. Part of the Hilton Hotels family, Hampton Inn finds themselves in a highly competitive space. The Internet has commoditized the hotel industry. Clean and comfortable rooms abound and where you find one small hotel, you most often find several—and all competitively priced.

So, let's imagine that same strategic meeting among the Hilton/Hampton decision-makers: "We are a clean, comfortable option for vacationing families and cost-conscious business travelers. Then again, so are Holiday Inn Express, Comfort Inn, Fairfield Inn, and more. What do we offer that others do not?"

Today, when you walk into a room at a Hampton Inn, you will notice a yellow sticky note stuck to the headboard. It looks handwritten, but it is printed that way. It reads: "Duvet covers and sheets are clean for your arrival."

Alright, let's be candid for a minute. We've all seen those investigative hidden camera reports showing hotel rooms with a purple light revealing the various bodily fluids strewn about the room and covering the bedspreads. I'm not trying to be gross. People are disgusting and all of that is no more evident than in what they do in hotel rooms. The Hampton team recognized a newly-discovered concern; they found a way to address the problem, they weighed the costs involved, and created a distinct and hygienic competitive advantage. If you don't want to worry about sitting on someone else's DNA, Hampton Inn is a safe bet.

Once again, there are costs to be weighed. The hotel housekeepers might only be able to clean perhaps 14 rooms a day instead of 15. The laundry costs will rise by some measure and they have to educate customers about the new policy/benefit. But those small, tangible costs can be offset by winning more business—and that's the point, isn't it? When all things are equal in the minds of your prospects, what can you offer to tip the scales in your favor? Because Hampton Inn added value—in this case, confidence in their cleanliness—it has become a better choice among a sea of good choices for those where cleanliness is a concern.

You don't have to be the best choice for everyone, but certainly for your core market segment.

Duluth Trading Company, known for their comfortable workwear, solved the age-old problem of T-shirts and other work shirts staying tucked in when bending over or reaching up. Their clever and irreverent television commercials illustrate this benefit by showing animated workmen offering up a little too much "carpenter crack." Point made—and remembered! In a vast sea of good choices, they are a better choice for those who identify with this problem. Their approach makes them stand out. And it's not just clever messaging and delivery; they actually produce a better product for the reasons they claim.

The point, once again, is that everyone is good and before we even look at effective messaging, we have to discover, uncover, or create a reason to be a better choice. Sometimes, it's right under our nose and only with a little distance can we truly see it. Other times, it must be envisioned, created, revised, implemented, launched, and promoted.

In addition to Volvo owning the "safe car" and Nordstrom owning "retail customer service," Wal-Mart has the lowest prices, Las Vegas owns debauchery, Apple owns technology innovation, IKEA reinvented furniture shopping, Harley Davidson owns "bad-ass" motorcycle riders, and Domino's is the king of pizza delivery.

What category can you own? This is a scenario where nuance can often be the deciding factor when you are competing in a crowded category. You don't have to be the best choice for everyone, just your targeted segment. You might be the best place for ribs in Overland Park Kansas, the cheapest place to get your car painted in south Florida, or the best jazz band in Syracuse, NY. Big fish in small ponds is a proven success model.

Emerging as the "next best thing" can be effective, but it's often fleeting. Anyone can do the next iteration, incremental improvements, or add new flavors. Profound marketing opportunities exist when you create products and services that do more than merely replicate or slightly enhance, but do so in an exponential or profound way. If you have the opportunity, be bold! Be uber-creative and develop offerings that are truly market-changing. Rethink problems. Change the game and you can be more than merely good, you can be impossible to ignore.

Then there are the market-changers who truly disrupt their categories. Few will replicate their success, but we can all glean lessons from the case studies. True innovators take a step (or a hundred steps) back and look for entirely new solutions to longstanding problems.

With the original iPod, Apple allowed us to buy single songs instead of albums. Not only could we buy a song instantaneously and without driving to the record store, we no longer needed crates or other storage devices. The iPod allowed us to store thousands of songs on a small device.

Uber has shaken the taxi industry to its core, by saying to themselves, "Why do people need to look for or wait for a professional driver to take them where they want to go? There are millions of cars on the road. Maybe one of those cars can pick them up." And despite protests from angry cab drivers and others, that genie will never go back in the bottle.

When a vastly improved service delivery model or product emerges, behaviors change. Netflix killed Blockbuster, but not because Blockbuster did a poor job. A better way was found and people don't often look back. It's not personal. It's human nature.

Products to dry your hands in public restrooms have been a shifting industry. For decades, the disease-ridden, rotating hand towel offered false comfort for those heeding the call to wash their hands after doing their business. The disposable paper towel was a welcome upgrade, but often expensive for venue owners and managers. The real revolution came from air. The wall-mounted electric hand dryer was a game-changer in the 1970s. Blowing hot air to dry hands without having to buy or wash towels was a one-time cost and an adequate if not perfect solution. The downside was the anemic dryer's fan. It didn't blow hard and drying your hands under the dryer was slow. People often left before their hands were truly dry, wiping their moist hands on their pants.

Enter the Xlerator in the year 2000. You've seen this brushed, aluminum hand dryer mounted on the wall in public restrooms with the simple, round opening at the bottom. It doesn't just blow harder, it blows so much harder than a traditional hand dryer that it has created an entirely new category. The creators asked the question: "What don't people like about traditional hand dryers?" Duh! They don't blow hard enough. So, what's the point of creating just another hand dryer if you can't make it significantly better? There's no WTV value there.

The company certainly could have created an incrementally better dryer and would likely have scored sales, but not many conversations. "Our current dryers are fine," facility managers would say. It's hard to justify a new expenditure for something that doesn't make my life, or that of my audience, significantly better. But with a revolutionary dryer that blows 10 times as hard, the Xlerator has become impossible to ignore.

The Air Blades are another example of rethinking the hand dryer quandary and have seen great success. Their next challenge, however, is to maintain the same level of effectiveness, but with a wider opening. I know we are all a little worried about accidentally touching the sides. Careful . . . careful . . . damn!

Dyson tackled the challenge of creating a vacuum that doesn't lose suction by rethinking where the dust and dirt go and the path to take it there. Tesla set their sights beyond being "as good as" a gasoline-powered car and asked an unexpected question: "Can we create an electric car that's not just as good as a regular car, but actually better?"

Architects and contractors from around the globe came together in Dubai tasked with constructing the tallest building in the world. Knowing that it would be surpassed shortly after construction, they committed to creating a building so tall that no one could catch up for many years. At 2,722 feet and over half a mile high, the Burj Khalifa in Dubai is nearly twice the height of the Willis (Sears) Tower in Chicago. It isn't just newsworthy, it is impossible to ignore.

The key is to huddle with your team and ask the question, "What can we be the best choice for?" and be honest with yourself about what is achievable. Do you have the time, discipline, personnel, and resources to win at whatever you identify? Then go about putting the pieces into place. Once again, before we start delving into messaging, marketing, and other promotions, make sure you have something worth promoting!

Often, we resort to knocking our competitors in order to have something to talk about and build ourselves up in the minds of our prospects. Some of our biggest criticisms are aimed at the largest players in the category. The behemoths are easy targets for their lack of flexibility, cumbersome decision-making process, onerous contracting and payment systems, and perceived impersonal approach. But let's call a spade and spade: they are bigger than you for a reason! They make more money than you. They employ more people than you. Clearly, they are doing something right.

We have to be very careful denigrating competitors—large or small. To be fair, I am a big proponent of "calling out" competitors when speaking with prospects. It's the proverbial "elephant in the room." Your prospects know that they have options. Call it out, but don't ever trash your competitors. Call out meaningful differentiation, but not by making yourself look petty or unethical.

If there is a service or feature they do not offer, it's not because "they don't care about the little guy," or "they don't care about special orders." It is just because it's not their business model. You can accomplish the same strategy of highlighting the limitations of a competitor. Just don't question their integrity. Merely remind them that others can't or won't meet their specific or custom needs because it is not their business model.

One sales approach I really like is to bring up a major competitor when meeting with or talking to a prospect. List five or six things they do really well, but that you know your prospect doesn't need:

"Of course, XYZ Company is the biggest player. They are great if you need A, B, C, D, or E. But X is all we do. We have built infrastructure and staffing and offer products and services to deliver X better than anyone else."

In other words, paint competitors as generalists and yourself as a specialist. There will be more specific sales and marketing language approaches later in the book.

So, let's look at your competition.

Exercise: "Buzzword Bingo" Side-By-Side Comparison

Gather all of your marketing materials—everything you've written about yourself—your brochures, sales sheets, catalogues, collateral, website page, and more and print them off and spread them out on a big table. Now, take all the promotional materials of your top three competitors—their sales sheets, ads, catalogues, brochures, and so on. If you don't have all of these on hand, you are operating at a deficit! Go out and secret-shop your competitors. Pretend to be a prospect and ask them to send you their promotional material. You will find that they actually give this stuff away for free!

When you have all of your competitors' materials printed off, spread them out along side yours and mix them up. Then, give a different colored highlighter to key members of your team and have everyone walk around that table and play what I call "Buzzword Bingo." Highlight key phrases, claims, and assertions about your quality, commitment, trust, service, passion, and people from your material and that of your competitors. Chances are you will be stunned by the similarities, if not outright word-for-word identical claims made by both you and your competitors! You will likely think that they plagiarized you—as they would believe the same of you, if they took the time to do this. They probably won't.

Before you go out and start promoting what you think makes you a great choice, you need to be confident that others are not promoting the same attributes. It's time for a little overt and covert investigation.

Spend a couple of weeks researching your competitors. Now, to be clear, even if no others do exactly what you do, but simply professes to solve the same problem in their own unique way, they are your competitor! If they are a choice for me, then they are a competitor of yours.

Pose as a customer and shop your competition— literally. If it is reasonable to do so, even buy what they are selling. Dine in their restaurant, have them service your car, stay in their hotel, or have them groom your trees. If the purchase is high-end, or a complicated sales-cycle endeavor, go through the process. Send away for their materials, call them on the phone, and sit through their presentation.

You are not wasting their time. You are doing them a favor! The more you are able to differentiate yourself and make yourself a better choice for your audience, the more you can relegate them to pick another lane and find success elsewhere.

The point is: how do you know how best to compete against your competitors, until you are clear how they are competing against you? Most tend to market with blinders on. Your prospects are being bombarded with sales and marketing messages from your competitors and they are not asking themselves whether or not to do business with you. They are deciding amongst a slew of qualified choices to get their needs met.

So, who wins? The winner is the one who is top-of-mind and stands out for a reason that is meaningful to the prospect. The good news is there are a myriad of ways to stand out, but you'll never do so by merely highlighting competency, qualifications, people, and service.

Ask yourself, "Who in my category is winning and on what?" Despite what some might teach, you have to compare yourself to others in your space. Decide where you want to compete and where you will defer. Just because one player might be the "low price leader," doesn't mean you have to play that game.

You might be the most luxurious, approachable, reliable, awarded, innovative, high-profile, expensive (yes, that can be an advantage), lightest, fastest, longest-lasting, longest-serving, most experienced, and more. You might focus your attention on solving an age-old problem, or on enhancing your logistics to offer the fastest delivery.

A simple caution: in your quest for differentiation, be careful not to reduce your target market too much. If you become the best choice for a very limited market, then you're taking a big gamble. Not only is your prospective market limited, but you are vulnerable from a lack of diversification. In other words, if all your eggs are in one basket, the basket (premise) better hold up.

Kota Longboards had a less-than-successful encounter with business turnaround specialist Marcus Lemonis on the phenomenal CNBC show *The Profit*. With his very expensive, high-quality longboards, the owner targeted the ultra-limited, exclusive, and questionable skateboarding demographic of "45–65-year-old skateboarders."

"Did you just make up this demographic?" famed skateboarder Rob Dyrdek asked with dismay. "Do you just not want to do well?"

In the interest of full disclosure, I own two Kota Longboards and they are phenomenal and so fun to ride with my son! These long skateboards are everything they claim and more. The problem is that there are not enough of "me" and my demographic to sustain the business and support the pricing and targeting strategy.

The mistake that too many in business make is they assume that what they like is exactly what the marketplace will like. Worse yet, they support their delusion by surrounding themselves with friends and family who agree with their ideas, but never get an accurate feel for the market. They release an ice cream flavor that they love, but never do market testing. They decide to bottle and sell their odd family recipe spaghetti sauce that they grew up with, but it tastes weird to others who don't share their history or nostalgia.

The lesson is that there is a place in business for trusting your gut, but not when it comes to ultra market segmentations. Test your assumptions. Go beyond your circle for real data and prove your concept before going all in.

In this age where we no longer have any unmet needs, too often companies look to create products and services that are more in the "want" than "need" categories. Both approaches can be successful, but when money is tight, the "need" always gets the cash. There is a reason that toilet paper will always be recession-proof.

There are great examples, however, where new "needs" were created. Some successful examples include: the hand sanitizer (how have we survived for thousands of years without it?), bottled water (if you had told people a generation ago that they would pay for water like they pay for soda, they'd have thought you were crazy), "nanny cams" (are caregivers really hurting our children en mass?), and more.

Occasionally, creative "geniuses" try to create a need where one might not have been perceived previously. Products are always coming to market with questionable premises offering solutions that are just looking for a problem. Fit Vegetable Spray is trying to convince us that we are not getting our vegetables clean with water in the sink. I'm not buying it—figuratively or literally. Then there is "Sexy Beast" dog perfume, or there is this underwear with a built-in smell eliminator. (Yeah, we'll just use a washing machine. Thanks, though.)

Business start-up television shows like *Shark Tank*, *Bar Rescue*, and *The Profit* do a great job of holding entrepreneurs' feet to the fire—not just in terms of the business model, logistics, finances, and quality, but the actual need for the products and how they are perceived within the context of a competitive marketplace. Most will ask the question: "Why is this product or service better than the alternatives currently available?" For others, however, the issue is: "Why would I even buy something like this at all?" It's not even an issue of "fad" or "need." Many dumb ideas will never even make it to "fad" status.

The naming of products is also an important discipline and can either bolster or hamper your efforts. We live in a time where market research is a mere click away. Honestly, you have no excuse to not research your competitors, your category, customers, and more. What is working and what isn't?

Too often in recent years, companies and organizations have suffered false starts as they promote a new brand, name, or slogan only to find out it's owned or used by another. A simple Google search would have uncovered the duplication, but people become so enamored with their brilliant ideas, assuming they were the first to come up with it.

For example, I own the trademark for the term "Visibility Coach." I have used it as my moniker and for my business interests for well over a decade and went through the trouble and expense of registering the federal trademark to ensure I could build my brand without duplication or confusion.

However, a simple Google search and scheduled alerts inform me on a fairly regular basis that someone has infringed on my moniker. What's so disturbing is that too often it is a competitor playing in the same sandbox of professional speaking, business consulting, or executive coaching and they jump into the market calling themselves a "Visibility Coach," or worse yet, *The* Visibility Coach. Um . . . no. I am The Visibility Coach and I own the trademark. Stand down!

To be fair, most are innocent mistakes made by overeager professionals who were probably having a cup of coffee when the epiphany hit them.

"I've got it!" they exclaim. "I'm a Visibility Coach!"

"That's brilliant!" their friends exclaim.

Yep. It is brilliant and my friend and colleague Eric Chester and I came up with it nearly 15 years ago. A quick Google search would have shown dozens of pages with the term—all about me.

I have sent "cease and desist" letters to at least a dozen professionals, many of whom had recently built websites, recorded video, and even created products, all using my trademarked term without an easy Google search to see if it was taken. Inexcusable! Or, at the very least, it is lazy. It's not like you have to drive to the library or send an information request to the Trademark Office. Just grab your smartphone and search it. It's basic.

Brainstorm ideas with your team, but then do the required research to make sure that your idea is "own-able." Sure, a lot of great ideas are taken, but millions of ideas are still out there. Do the work!

In crafting your verbiage, once again, be sure to dig deep into your industry and your competitors. If you offer essentially what others do, we don't know what makes you better unless you tell us something different or use different claims and descriptors. Use your online research to do more than merely look for clever terms. Search for a unique value proposition, differentiating product mix, service delivery model, persona, amenities, and so on. It's a lot easier to describe something that is genuinely different in your business than to find a different way to describe things that are essentially the same.

CHAPTER 3

Discover Your Competitive Advantages

Imagine you are sitting across from a large prospect, negotiating a sale. What would you normally say to close the deal? What is your standard spiel, mantra, or approach? (Granted, I can't really know your specific business model, but play along.)

Now, let's alter the scenario: you are sitting across from an important prospect. You *have to* make this sale. In fact, if you don't make this sale, you'll have to close part of your business and lay off half of your workforce. You will miss your business loan payment to the bank and fail to make your mortgage payment. You will be unable to pay the tuition for your children's school and your marriage will teeter on the brink.

Now, what would you say and do to land this client or make this sale? How deep would you go and how hard would you work? When failure is not an option, we find a way.

I would suggest that if you are in business, failure is not an option. If it is, then you are not "all in." You don't have the commitment necessary to win at this game. If failure is an option, then you have no right hiring people and promising them a livelihood. Sure, failure in business happens all too often. You just can't approach it with an acceptance of that eventuality. You shouldn't approach your marketing with a casual approach either. There is too much at stake and wolves are at the gate.

I was coaching a CEO who was becoming burnt out on her business. She had been working to build a very cool company, but was becoming disillusioned about how long it was taking. She enjoyed her work and the socially conscious benefit it was having in an impoverished part of the world where she sourced her materials, but was not sure she could keep her attention for the estimated four to five years it would take to build the distribution network to really grow the revenue for herself and her investor.

"Honestly," she said to me candidly, "I don't think I can stay in this mode for anything beyond two more years." I asked if there was any way she could accelerate the work and motivate her team to get it done in only two years?

"No way," she responded shaking her head. "There's no way we could get it done that fast."

I said, "Okay, humor me here. Imagine someone said to you: 'If you can't get it done in two years, you will contract a life-threatening illness and leave your children without a mother.' Could you figure out a way?"

"Well, of course I could!" she said with a smile. "I would find a way."

"Tell me how you would do it if your very life was on the line," I instructed.

For the next 10 minutes, she laid out a brilliant and unconventional plan and detailed the steps she would take to accomplish the distribution and expansion. In addition, she laid out a scenario to create the necessary supporting infrastructure and staffing growth within a very doable two-year time frame.

"Wow! I guess I can do it," she said, marveling at her own ingenuity, and punching me in the arm for making her face her mortality.

Here's the point: you likely have reasonable, but not great marketing efforts and marketing messages because you have focused your efforts on your product or service quality and delivery. You tend to blend in with others in your industry because you have allowed yourselves to blend in. Don't beat yourself up over it. It got you to where you are. Just commit to working harder and going deeper if you want to go farther. Remember, getting new business is not about competency, it's about competitive advantage.

We are all looking for new clients, new customers, and increased sales. You are mistaken, however, if you think your biggest marketing challenge is acquiring new customers. The truth is that most of your prospects are already getting their needs met by another company, professional, resource, or in some other way. Most people are perfectly happy with their current provider.

I often hear business leaders or sales professionals lament the challenges of acquiring new customers or clients. Your real challenge in business is not to *acquire* new customers or clients—it's to *convert* someone else's customer into your customer. That's hard! They are likely getting their needs met right now. You have to help them understand how they are being underserved, overcharged, or settling for less. You have to convince people that they have a problem they didn't know they had, rip open that wound, pour some salt on it, and offer yourself as the medicine—a better option.

Often, our biggest challenge in sales is engaging with prospects who are simply "fine." They kind of like where they are and see no real need to change. "Nah, I'm good," they say. Even when we know what we are offering is a better choice, if they don't see it as better, or enough of an improvement over their current situation, then they will not be inspired to move.

You see this dynamic played out across the country when it comes to the local television news battles. Local news stations spend millions of dollars upgrading their *Super Double Doppler Extreme 5000* weather tracker, and hire away top talent, while offering an endless stream of late-breaking "Team Coverage" of the first snowflake of the season. All of this is done in an effort to get people to switch from the news team they already like to the one they rarely watch. And although a station may win an Emmy Award for the best newscast, most people will stick with their favorite. They watch them because they like them. They have to have a reason to switch and your awards often aren't enough to leave their familiar news team.

So, if the challenge is actually harder than you realized, how do you expect to complete a more difficult task with the same strategy you have been using for years? Visibility marketing isn't just about sending your message out there; it's about having a better message out there and everywhere your prospects are.

The questions growing businesses struggle with are: Can you do great marketing without an expensive firm? Can you and your current team do this work? Most of the time, the answer is "yes," as long as you don't shortchange the process. You have to work harder at this than you have been. Treat yourself like a client and give this effort the time and attention it deserves! You have to do a deeper dive.

Traditional marketing claims still dominate the business landscape, but are simply no longer effective. Still very common, but essentially worthless marketing claims include:

- "Our people make the difference!"
  (Your people bear a striking resemblance to the people that work for your competitors.)
- "We use only the freshest ingredients."
  (Um, you're serving me food! What is the alternative? "We use nearly expired

ingredients, but pass the savings on to you!")

- "See what it's like to do business with people who love what they do." (Nope. Not buying it.)
- "Honesty, integrity, and trust." (So, you're telling me that you are not going to cheat me. You're telling me this.)
- "We are passionate about X." (Passion is one of the most overused and least effective words in modern marketing. Have passion, talk about it internally, but stop using it in your marketing.)
- "We really listen to our clients." (How else are you staying in business? Everyone listens to their customers and clients. Everyone!)
- "Our customers come first!" (Honestly, I have no idea what this means.)
- "We have over 320 years of combined experience." (When you make me do math, I don't hear the next five things you say because I'm busy . . . doing math.)

The first step is to admit that you have a problem. See where you fall into these traps. Then, move beyond "competency" claims and dig deeper pointing to differentiation, preference, and legitimate competitive advantage.

When Wendy's hamburgers put the slogan "Quality is our recipe!" on the side of their business in permanent letters right under their logo, they wasted a golden opportunity to tell us why they are a better choice than all of the other restaurants on the same block. Instead, their claim is beyond dismissible and borders on ridiculous.

In fact, any claim of superior service, people (that make the difference), great taste, or honest employees falls on deaf ears. I'm not suggesting that your claims aren't true, they're just the same as everyone else's claims and nobody is buying it. Your current customers might agree, but your prospective ones don't.

Admittedly, crafting descriptive verbiage is more of an art than a science, but as art, it deserves time and collaboration to be both creative and persuasive. Remember my example from the beginning of the book about the Super Bowl commercials? Companies can be creative if they take the time to dig deep and do it right. The good news for you is that most won't.

When crafting the words you use to describe yourself, one of the worst strategies employed by so many hapless marketing firms and advertising agencies is to interview and survey your current customers and clients to discover "the truth about what really sets you apart from the only people who really matter—your customers." They go out and survey them to ask why they do business with you and the results are often meaningless. The problem is they pitch this high-priced "process" to their clients and their clients get garbage. Why? *Because the reason that customers do business with you and stay with you is rarely the same reason they came to you in the first place!*

Happy customers will say that they love the relationships they've built with you. Unfortunately, touting the great relationship to someone who has not done business with you, has no relationship with you, and just needs a reasonably priced product or service is a wasted claim.

A financial planning firm hired a Web design firm to redo their online presence. These Web guys also fancied themselves "marketing geniuses" and convinced the firm to let them re-do their messaging as well. But instead of doing the hard work required to understand the competitive landscape and come up with a persuasive marketing campaign, they surveyed the firm's clients for their ideas. They sent out some variation of "What words would you use to describe this financial planning firm?" The long-term clients used many words to describe their positive relationship with the firm principals and staff. The agency came back and proclaimed that the answer revealed itself! "You are: fun, energetic, and dynamic!" Yep, they built the promotional campaign around those three words.

Um . . . a financial planning firm is fun, energetic, and dynamic? That be may be so for the long-term clients. These people have built relationships and trust through months and years and enjoy being able to let their hair down a bit and develop genuine friendships with their clients. But if you were a business owner with fairly complex tax issues and arduous compliance requirements, or a high net-worth individual with a change in their investment environment, would you look for a financial firm that was fun, energetic, and dynamic? Hell no! You would want one with a deep bench of knowledge, specialized experience with your industry, and a strong track record of successfully navigating complex tax and compliance issues similar to yours.

I'm not suggesting falling in line with pedestrian claims of expertise, perspective, integrity, and vision, among others, but at least it's a safer direction and aligned with the criteria people use when hiring professional service providers to manage their affairs.

If they wanted to use worthless claims for a financial services firm like fun, energetic, and dynamic, they might as well have just said they love puppies, are allergic to latex, and prefer crunchy peanut butter.

Marketing firms, ad agencies, and other professionals pull this crap all the time. Lazy! That's why most of the commercials you see on TV can't be recalled 30 seconds after they air, don't move you to buy anything, and only serve to further relegate the business to a meaningless bucket of commodity.

The primary purpose of most marketing efforts is simply to get "up to bat" with prospects. Most of us can convert the lion share of prospects we can get in front of. The real challenge is to come up with the right words and approaches to get an audience with a prospect. The initial claims in your marketing, or other outreach, is to move prospects toward agreeing to the first, in-person exchange. If you can get in front of your prospects, you are going to close a lot of those deals. Are the words you are choosing accomplishing that goal? Do your words make someone say "That's what I've been looking for. Finally someone gets it! Let's meet."?

I heard a comedian once who said that he saw a van with the words "Creative Electric" on the side and he was thinking to himself: "Uh, I don't think I want my electrician to be creative! I want him to do it the way it's supposed to be done!"

Funny to be sure, but he makes a good point. Words matter. You have to choose words that create the image that is going to move a prospect toward you and not away. It's easy to be a nonconformist, but why be different for the sake of being different? The key is not just to be different, but to be better! To win the battle, the words have to be effective in moving people from information to action.

Ad agencies and marketing firms use the flawed "survey the clients" approach because it makes sense to their clients as a strategy and makes it appear as if there is a data-driven, calculated process being used to develop the strategy. To be clear, I am not knocking legitimate market research; it can yield some truly valuable insights and information. I'm saying that having clients' customers dictate your marketing messages based on what they like about you is both lazy and ineffective. Did I mention that it is lazy?

You may go to a grocery store because of proximity and convenience. Maybe there was a sale that brought you in. You stay because it is familiar, you know the layout, and can get in and out quickly.

You go to a restaurant for the first time because it's on the way, you have a coupon, your friends suggest it, or you read a positive review. You come back because you enjoyed the food and the ambiance, the prices were fair, and you had a great time.

Instead of asking customers what they like about you, find out why they came to you in the first place. Why did they come in for the first time or why did they agree to take a meeting?

A professional colleague and close friend that I have known and worked with for 20 years asked me once: "Do you know why I hired you originally? I called your office and you said to me, 'Give me a second to get something off my desk so I can give you my undivided attention.'" Armed with that feedback, you can bet that I used that approach again and again.

Another colleague of mine offers executive coaching and when she is meeting a prospect for the first time, she opens the conversation with: "There is a reason why you agreed to meet with me. Let's start there." Brilliant!

To be clear, it's always good to keep the lines of communication open and important to gauge customer satisfaction. Armed with what clients like and don't like about working with you, you are able to make course corrections, provide enhanced value, and retain your best customers. Marketing, on the other hand, is different. I tell my clients that retaining customers is their business. Helping them attract new customers is mine.

The better strategy is to ask yourself (or work closely with your team or hired guns to ask): What problem do you solve better than anyone else? What can we offer that no one else has . . . yet? Are we the most acclaimed, recognized, referred, searched, mentioned, purchased, visited, or referenced? What have we done more often than others, have more expertise in, and have more beneficial connections or industry knowledge?

Exercise: Why Customers Buy

List all the reasons why someone would buy something you are selling—not buy from you specifically, but why they would buy the item or service in general.

For example, if you own a Mexican restaurant, you might say: "People go to a Mexican restaurant because":

- People are hungry.
- They like Mexican food.
- They are in the mood for something different.
- Someone suggests Mexican food.

Now, list why you think people choose you over other alternatives:

- They have been here before and they like us.
- We are close to their home or office.
- We have faster service than the other restaurants in our vicinity.
- We provide a more authentic experience than competing Mexican restaurants.
- We offer a "kids eat free" special on Tuesdays and Wednesdays.
- We have a more visible location.
- We sponsor the local baseball team.
- We know many of them by name.

And finally, discover and list why they came in for the first time:

- They saw an ad.
- Referred by a friend or an online review.
- Had a coupon or saw an advertised special.

- Spur of the moment decision and felt like Mexican food and was driving by.

Now, here is the hard part. Create the same list for your two nearest competitors. Why do people choose them? Be honest and complimentary. (Remember, people shop your competitors because they like them. They chose them!)

Their list might include:

- Their American food is more familiar.
- They have chicken nuggets and kids always want chicken nuggets.
- They have salad choices.
- They have gluten-free and vegetarian options.
- They have a better sign out front.
- They do more advertising.

Are you getting the picture? It's easy to compete if you understand why people buy.

You have to market to two different audiences: For the ones who like you, you need to increase frequency. For the ones who don't know you, it's all about awareness and encouraging an initial trial. How might those two marketing messages differ?

When you understand your competition better and why people buy from them, then you can tailor your messages to influence them to choose you instead. You can also alter your value proposition if needed. Are there deficiencies in your product mix and/or service delivery that you can address? Are there more creative and effective ways of reaching prospects before they are ready to buy?

Ultimately, you are going to have to go after your competitors' customers if you are going to grow. Knowing what they do well is an important first step in luring them away. Having clarity about what makes you better is the foundation you'll need to plot your strategy.

CHAPTER 4

It's Not What You Want to Say, It's What They Want to Hear!

An old boss of mine used to say: "Son, when you put information out there without a clear idea of what you want them to do with it, it's like peeing in your pants. It'll give you a warm feeling for a minute, but it won't do you much good in the long run."

Businesses make money in three ways: get new customers (customer acquisition/conversion), get the current customers to come back more often (increased frequency), and get the current customers to buy more when they are already there (up-sell). Marketing campaigns need to effectively target all three behaviors and the strategy is different for each one.

For the new prospects, the goal is to elicit an initial trial, incentivize them to come in, call, or try you for the first time. Remember, you can't have a repeat customer if you don't have a first-time customer.

For current or previous customers, you need to remind them of why they liked you or to give them a reason to return. Kellogg's cereal had a great TV campaign where they stopped people on the street and gave them a bowl of Kellogg's Corn Flakes. People of course loved it and had this wonderful look of joy and nostalgia on their face. "Oh yeah. I love Corn Flakes!" they would say. "Kellogg's Corn Flakes," the announcement began, "taste them again for the first time." Getting out there and reminding people why they like you is a crucial part of visibility marketing.

For current customers, the strategy is different. The more we can sell them while they are in store, on the website, or on the phone, the more we maximize our profit. For existing clients, the customer acquisition costs are already accounted for; selling them more while they are on your website or your physical location is an art, and one that you would do well to master (more about up-selling in Chapter 5).

Let's talk first about new prospects.

Let's be clear about one thing: your prospective customers are not out there floundering around, desperate to find you. In fact, they are likely already getting their needs met, whether it is from a competitor or an alternative scenario. Regardless, few prospects are sitting and waiting for you. You have to be visible where they are. You need to go out and get them.

Compounding the visibility challenge is the reality that we are all bombarded with endless sales pitches and advertising messages throughout our day—every day. So, to break through the clutter, we have to be better. We have to be more strategic, more creative, and more persuasive.

There is a popular sales strategy that teaches to break up the sales process into small pieces. Often, it's much simpler to persuade someone to give a simple "yes" to a preliminary question, rather than a full commitment to the final sales. For example, it's easier to get a prospect to agree to meet for coffee than to sign a year-long contract. Once you're having coffee, you can move them closer to signing a contract.

You need to ask yourself, "What is the one simple activity that is predictive of ultimate sales success?" In other words, if you know that you can close 70 percent of the prospects you can meet with face to face, then gear your marketing to achieve that singular behavior.

In short, don't market to get the sale. Smart companies market to achieve the behavior that leads to the sale.

GEICO insurance bombards the airwaves with clever ads using its recognizable Gecko character among other creative and memorable offerings. What is interesting about GEICO is that they almost never ask you to buy their insurance. They just want one thing from you: 15 minutes.

It's a simple request. You have 24 hours in every day and over 18,000 minutes in every week. They just want 15 of those minutes. And, in exchange for those brief 15 minutes, you might save 15 percent or more on your car insurance. GEICO knows that getting you to agree to that one simple action is predictive of sales success. They have a very high closing rate for prospects they can get on the phone, so their ads are geared toward getting you to give them 15 minutes on the phone.

I would suggest that this is also true for most of us in business. If we can get a prospective customer or client to meet with us, come into our office, visit our restaurant, tour our timeshares, visit our website, listen to 20 seconds of a downloadable song, sample our cinnamon roll, and more, we have increased the likelihood of an actual sale exponentially!

Plastic surgeons aren't asking for a commitment to go under the knife—just to have you come in for a free consultation. Time-share peddlers dangle a free weekend in exchange for sitting through their 90-minute presentation. Car dealers offer a test drive. Mattress manufacturers encourage you to try it free for 30 days. Each small "yes" leads you closer to the desired sale. Then the key is to influence each behavior along the path. Your primary marketing task is marketing to elicit the first "contact" behavior.

Effective marketing today is often about the incremental sale. Although some benefit from the impulse buy, rarely will prospects commit to larger purchases quickly. To be clear, I'm not referring to customers and prospects who are already onsite, in your store, or at the point of sale. This is about getting them to that point. This is about a series of "yes's" on the way to the final "yes."

I helped to launch a chain of Brazilian Steakhouses in America in the late 1990s. I told my

PR team that we had one goal: to get them one customer, one time; and then, to get another customer one time, and another. Once that new customer walked through the front door of their restaurant, our work was done. At that point, the restaurant had better be as good as I told media outlets and others they were. Retention was their job. Talking about increasing frequency and teaching the staff about up-selling was a future conversation.

I speak for a living; I also consult and coach, but most of that work comes from people who see me delivering business branding keynote speeches. There is one behavior that has proven predictive of my success in generating bookings: a prospect must get a clear vision of what I offer. In fact, they need to actually see me doing what I do on stage.

My brilliant team at Visibility International knows that if we can get meeting planners, speakers' bureaus, and others who hire speakers, to go to my website at *www.visibilitycoach.com* and click on the preview video in the center of my homepage, then I have a good shot of getting the speaking gig. If they don't watch that video featuring clips of my speaking around the world, or they haven't seen me speak before, I have zero-chance of getting hired to speak. Nobody is going to book a speaker who they haven't seen speak. The risk is too high.

So, when someone on my staff has an idea for enhancing our marketing, we ask the question: "Is that idea more likely to get a meeting planner to click on that video?" And if the answer is "no," then we don't do it. Like you, we don't have unlimited time and resources. We are laser-focused on influencing the one behavior from our prospects that is predictive of our success: watching my preview video.

For many companies, being perceived as the safe choice and eliciting the behavior that leads to the sales are one and the same. A tactic that has proven effective across multiple industries is "sampling." Sampling answers the question: "Can you paint a compelling picture of how my life will be different if I buy from you?"

In its most recognizable form, sampling is a young worker standing among the shoppers in a food court directly in front of a Panda Express, holding a toothpick with a succulent piece of Orange Chicken (their number-one seller), and repeating "Sample? Sample?" to the shoppers who pass her way. Now, keep in mind that Panda Express is most often operating in one of the most competitive environments imaginable—a food court. Imagine how you might approach your business differently if your nearest competitor was only nine steps away. Oh, and your next competitor was nine more steps away and so on.

Panda Express has done the analytics. They know their customer acquisition costs and the currency is Orange Chicken. You say to yourself: "Hmm. I'm hungry. Sabarro might be good. Then again, Renzio has decent Greek food. Maybe Orange Julius might be okay. There is always McDonald's." But if you already have a piece of sweet and succulent Orange Chicken in your mouth, you know that it is going to be good. It is a safe choice in a sea of good choices. Plus, you are already enjoying it. More Orange Chicken would be good right now!

What would shopping at Costco or Sam's Club on a Saturday be without an endless array of morsels located through the back of the store? When vendors strike an agreement to get their new or unfamiliar food item into these big box retailers, they have to agree to a sampling program. It makes sense for people to want to try before they buy because it makes the purchase safer.

Admittedly, I will go to a grocery store and buy a food item that I haven't tried before if the packaging looks appetizing, and especially if I go to the store hungry. But let's be clear: I am not buying a 20 pound bag of something at Costco or

Sam's Club that I haven't tried! It's too big a risk. Sampling eliminates the risk.

So, how does that apply to your business? Sampling can take many forms: For new construction, it is a portfolio of pictures of successfully completed projects. A plastic surgeon will show before and after pictures. An artist will show their portfolio (online of course). Health clubs will give you a free 30-day trial. "Fragrance models" will give you a spritz of perfume on the wrist. A chiropractor will offer a free spinal exam and most trusted advisors will offer a free consultation. Sampling is marketing! Getting samples out to where your prospects are is visibility marketing.

Another way to be a safer choice for customers and clients is to align with a national brand. You can purchase and operate a franchise, sell nationally branded products, or have your products sold by others with a larger reputation.

The thousands of privately-owned campgrounds and RV parks scattered across North America have historically been a bit of the "Wild West"—sometimes both literally and figuratively. With a vast array of locales and amenities, it has always been a bit of a crap-shoot to pack up the car or camper and drive hundreds of miles, trusting the brochure or company rep on the phone. Before you arrived to your campsite, and possibly in the dark or in the rain, you never really knew if the spot would be as described with trees, water, privacy, and relatively clean. (I grew up camping in the Colorado mountains and my son and I still go every year!) I think we've all had some bad experiences with facilities that were not as described.

Like their more refined cousins in the hotel industry, the Internet has brought both visibility and transparency to the camping industry. Websites offer photos, videos, reviews, and maps. As much as we want to make a good decision, we are most often looking to avoid making a bad decision. If we can't view the actual slot or site we are reserving, or if the park looks "sketchy," there are countless other options and we will not take the chance.

When it comes to camping, national parks are an ever-present option for campers and hikers. In response, privately-owned campgrounds have had to raise their game to become a better option in a vast sea of good choices.

Many solo operators have found success joining forces with a national brand like KOA, or Yogi Bear's Jellystone Park Camp-Resorts. Leveraging a national brand through licensure or franchise offers many benefits—if the brand is strong. Jellystone Resorts has also found "riches in niches." They don't try to be all things to all people. Smart companies become the best choice for their key demographic, and in Jellystone's case, that's families with small children. If you are looking to "rough it" or find solitude, you want to go elsewhere.

Jellystone Resorts cater to families wanting to avoid the two words every parent dreads: "I'm bored!" The resorts aren't simply campgrounds and RV parks. Many offer resort-style water parks, activities, boating, hayrides, amusement park rides, family dining, activity pavilions, shopping, group outings, horseback riding, petting zoos, and of course, Wi-Fi!

National franchisee conventions for Jellystone owners offer a sea of trade show vendors demonstrating the latest in games, massive inflatable rides, water park amenities, TV-style game shows, food, laundry resources, pre-made cabins, T-shirts, and hundreds of other ideas to keep kids busy, families entertained, and the company coffers full.

The brand offers exposure for franchisees, the familiarity of the Warner Bros. cartoon characters Yogi Bear and Boo-Boo (yes, you just heard their voices in your head), professional graphics and signage, best practices gleaned from the various franchisees and, most of all, it offers families the assurance that the resorts meet company standards demanded by the franchisor. Although each park is different, there is a perception of a certain level of consistency. Jellystone is not everyone's cup of tea, but for millions of families with young children they are the perfect choice for an active, connected getaway.

The not-so-secret of success for Jellystone offers a broader lesson: offer the core of what others do, but in a unique way that is attractive to a distinct segment of the audience. Nobody succeeds with trying to be all things to all people. The key is not just being a good choice, but the best choice for your audience.

Jony Ive, famed design head at Apple, has said: "It's easy being different. What's hard is being better." What are you doing in your business so well that it would cause someone to actually talk about you to someone else? Some call it "going viral," others call it creating "buzz." Seth Godin calls it being "remarkable" or worthy of being remarked about. It's not about being good. It's about being so good, delivering marketing that is so visible, so memorable and repeatable, that you are impossible to ignore.

It's become fashionable to lament the dearth of creative ideas. *The reality is that we don't have a deficiency in creativity; we too often have a pervasive lack of courage.* Creative people in business are often reluctant to share creative ideas for fear of being shut down. They've been brought up in a corporate culture that pays lip service to creativity, but rewards the status quo.

There is an oft-shared scenario where a group of very young school children are asked: "Who can sing and dance?" Virtually all the hands shoot into the air. Then the same question is asked of a group of high schoolers and most avert their eyes and slouch into their chairs. We are taught at an early age that to put yourself out there is to risk social ostracism. We take risks at times, but they are well-calculated risks.

It's easy to spot a strong group facilitator. The strong facilitator rewards participation. They know that when they ask the group members to share their ideas, every suggestion gets written on the flip chart for all to see. It's validation that the idea has merit. As they say: "The behavior that is recognized and rewarded is the behavior that is repeated." If an idea is shared by a participant and not written down with the others, then the sharing shuts down quickly. Nobody wants to offer an idea publicly that is deemed unworthy.

The same dynamic has thrown an enormous wet blanket on most business marketing. The most creative, outrageous, out-of-the-box, and potentially game-changing ideas are rarely shared. There are certainly super-creative firms that foster an open dialogue, but even in those environments, the most creative ideas are sanitized or focus-grouped to death before the client ever sees or hears them.

Here's the hard truth: although collaboration is often beneficial, consensus kills creativity. It's the group decision-making process that is responsible for the death of most truly creative marketing ideas. Out-of-the-box ideas are floated, focused-grouped, and after everyone is heard, concerns are considered and we are assured that nobody will be offended or their comfort zone disrupted. The once-bold idea has now been sanitized to the lowest common denominator. It may be safe. It may check all the boxes and fit the industry norms, but the mere fact that it feels safe means it won't likely stand out. Standing out requires doing something different and unexpected.

When 81-year-old Clara Peller famously shouted "Where's the beef?" in a 1984 Wendy's TV commercial, a "buzzworthy" catch phrase and a star was born. It was unexpected, nontraditional, and very, very funny.

Kmart caused a real stir a few years ago when a television commercial aired featuring people declaring: "I just shipped my pants!" After a quick double take and a collective "What did he just say?" we realized that he said "shipped." It may not be to your taste, but it certainly got your attention and was memorable! I say, bravo!

Marketing professionals come up with great ideas all the time. Those ideas just rarely make it through the sanitizing gauntlet and see the light of day. I am not talking about shock for the sake of shock, but boldness and creativity for the sake of conversation, memorability, buzzworthiness and, ultimately, winning!

Companies have struggled for centuries with the elusive challenge of staying top-of-mind with their customers and prospects. Today, billions of dollars are spent (and too often wasted) in an effort to gain and retain top-of-mind status with clients. Most efforts fall short in these hyper-competitive times; it simply takes more to stand out and few do nearly enough.

Social media is a terrific resource, but not the Holy Grail purported by so many who clearly have a dog in the race. Social media can certainly be a valuable weapon in your arsenal of resources. Social media can accomplish, for mere pennies, what others spend hundreds of millions to achieve. It can achieve not just recognition, but engagement; not just awareness, but involvement; not just identification, but shared identity; and not just "pushed" messaging, but actual, two-way conversation and bolstered decision-making. You may not be getting that right now, but I will show you how savvy competitors are.

Despite what overeager marketing and Internet professionals tell you, social media doesn't replace sales and marketing—it amplifies it by providing an interactive element. Though the basic tenants of influencing behavior haven't changed through time, the tactics certainly have.

The recipe is simple, but it's not easy: *if you want people to be interested, you have to be interesting!* There it is, both simple and profound, but it is the truest statement in this book. It's not about whether you have a blog or have a presence on the top social media platforms. It's about *being interesting* on your blog, Facebook, YouTube, Vine, SnapChat, Instagram, Twitter, Pinterest, or your TV and radio ads.

The problem for many is that the message gets lost for the messenger. Sometimes, you can't get out of your own way because you are far too focused on what you want to say as opposed to what your prospect needs to hear to get them to buy. This dynamic is no more evident than when your message is mission-based and your offering is not.

There is a generation of entrepreneurs who are approaching business with a noble cause. They have invented a vegan dog food because they don't believe in killing animals. They sell hand-crafted jewelry to provide a livelihood for disadvantaged villagers, or paintings to highlight the plight of refugees. And though the causes are noble, the market will always be limited by the marketing.

I spoke to a gentleman who was interested in some marketing assistance for his portable, solar-powered generators. These well-crafted items provided power in remote locations for campers, concerts, trade shows, street fairs, tiny houses, and even so-called "Dooms-Day Preppers." They're pretty cool power generators to be sure.

Unfortunately, visitors to the website were inundated with his personal crusade to save the planet. He pointed to the mission to reduce greenhouse gas emissions, provide sustainable options to fight global warming, and encourage a shift in our thinking about how we take care of our Mother Earth.

It's a noble cause to be sure, but what about the majority of potential customers who don't share his beliefs or priorities? It's not that people don't care about the planet; it's that we all pick the causes that are important to us and most, quite frankly, have other priorities. Put another way: our job is not to help this guy fulfill his mission.

The assumption too often with those who are on a crusade is that if they just explain it enough, they can get others to agree with them. During our first conversation, I asked him bluntly if his company was a 501-c-3 not-for-profit organization. "No," he said somewhat surprised. "We are an energy company."

"Then why all the preaching about your cause?" I asked.

"Well, that's why I started the company," he responded, "to make an impact."

"But what does that have to do with the trade show booth I want to power at the state fair?" I asked.

Trying to respect his views, I made it clear that only a fraction of his prospective customers were going to buy because they wanted to join his crusade to save the Earth. Most prospects are simply looking for quality power solutions that will work well in remote locations, without the noise of a generator or the smell of fumes. Many may even like the appearance of supporting responsible power generation, but they are buying for reasons that work for them.

Most of his messaging, or at least the up-front content, was aimed at less than 10 percent of his prospective customers. Some 90 percent don't care about his mission, but would love his products. I'm not suggesting that you bury your values, but just don't lead with them if they are irrelevant to your audience.

The "About Us" tab on your website should be about your credentials and not your story, unless your story is meaningful to the buyers. If you sell potato soup and it was your grandmother's recipe from the old country, then tell that story! If you have a charity to help injured dogs and you came from a war-torn region and saw animals being blown up by landmines, then by all means share that powerful story.

But if you started a technology company because you pulled yourself up by your bootstraps after surviving cancer, sorry, but who cares? It's a powerful story, sure, but completely irrelevant to your buyers. Take that Webpage and instead tell of your education, past experience with technology giants, or 30 years in the field.

Remember, in marketing, it's not what we want to say, it's what they want to hear! What we want to say is not unimportant. It's that we are competing for customers, and whoever speaks to their needs best, wins. The people looking for remote power options have endless choices. Most have already left the room before he got past his mission. They've already moved on to someone who understood their needs.

Your challenge is to "out-wordsmith" your competitors. The good news is that they tend to fall into the same traps as everyone else does touting their quality, commitment, caring, people, and so on.

Exercise: The Top 10 List (Solo or With Your Team)

Take out a piece of paper and number down the left side from one to 10, leaving room between the lines for a few sentences.

Give yourself 15 minutes and create a list of 10 persuasive statements and claims you can make about your business, service, or signature product that if your prospects knew, remembered, and believed, they would do business with you. In fact, if they knew and believed these claims, then they would feel stupid doing business with anyone else. Can you come up with 10?

This is the proverbial "gun to the head" exercise. Imagine you were writing a radio commercial for your business, or maybe you are on the phone with a prospect. The fact is that you have to land this client! You have to convince this customer to buy from you or you will have to fire half of your staff. Once again, what would you say? How deep would you go?

Here a few rules and guidelines:

- No slogans or pithy phrases.
- Make the sentences things you would say verbally. Don't write brochure copy; make it conversational.
- Don't simply list what you sell. It is a given that those elements will be a part of your marketing conversation.
- Brag a little! You are doing good work. There is no shame in claiming your territory.
- It doesn't have to be short or concise. Make it meaningful and persuasive!

Here are some examples:

Sole Claim: "We are the only company that . . ."

Action Verb: "We created, developed, pioneered . . ."

Supremacy: "We were the first, fastest, largest, oldest, softest . . ."

Honors: Named "Entrepreneur of the Year," "Best Place to Work," "Top 10 Supplier," "Vendor of the Year."

Media Appearances: "Perhaps you saw our front page article in . . ."

Key Clients: "Out of over 250 vendors, Macy's chose us as their exclusive . . ."

Innovation: "It's been done the current way for over 100 years; we have created a better model that allows . . ."

Dominance: "We have successfully installed more water heaters in the tri-state area than all of our competitors combined!"

Experience/Resilience: "We have been in business for over half a century and have watched competitors come and go. There is a reason we are still here."

Competitive Advantage: "Everyone else is still doing it the old way; you can gain an advantage over your competitors by working with us to . . ."

Swagger: "Honestly, with our current lineup and industry accolades, I wouldn't want to compete against us."

If you are working with your team, have everyone come up with their own list. Tee this up by saying: "I know what I think makes us great. I want to know what you think makes us great. Not simply what makes us capable, qualified, competent, and a good choice, but what makes us a better choice than the other capable, qualified, and competent competitors."

When everyone is done with their list, grab a flip chart and write down the great ideas and suggestions from your team. I guarantee you there is brilliance in the room. Your people live on the front lines every day. Tap their insights!

Now, evaluate and discuss the responses. As is often true, the real value is in the discussions and exploration. Begin to narrow down the best statements and claims. Ask yourselves: could one of these responses be used by competitors? If it could, then cross it off the list. Does it merely point to capacities that others share? Cross it off. Is it a vague, subjective claim of quality, service, or caring? Yep. Cross it off.

Agree on the best 10 on the list. Make them conversational and repeatable—not to be read as a list, but as talking points to infuse into your conversations.

Now comes the hard part: reduce it again to the top five. What are the five things that when communicated articulately, persuasively, and enthusiastically, would turn any prospect into a customer? You will likely get disagreement on the best five and that is okay. It means that your people are engaged! Ultimately, a decision must be made.

When you have settled on the five best claims, statements, assertions, and competitive advantages, take that list, shrink it down, print it out, laminate it, and then stick it to every phone in your business. Tape it to every person's desk and give an extra one for their wallet. The rule is that nobody gets off the phone or has a conversation with a prospect without saying three of those five things—every conversation, every time! I don't care if your kids are calling, or it is a wrong number, you are going to say at least three of those five statements.

The point is that if you are going to influence how you are described in the marketplace by prospects, partners, vendors, and more, then you have to have a hand in crafting the words you want others to use. This is not a passive exercise! It is an active one. Through exercises such as this one, you can drive the narrative. You can spoon-feed the words you want others to use and, by sheer repetition, you can influence their behavior. Of course, you can do it with your slogans and tag lines, but if you want to actually change the conversation, you have to craft the words and highlight the parts of your business that you want others to talk about.

CHAPTER 5

The Most Profitable Sales and Marketing Tactic—By Far!

Once again, there are three ways to increase your revenue: sell to more people, sell more to the people you already sell to, and get them to buy more often. But there is a not-so-subtle convergence that occurs at the point of purchase that allows you to often sell more to new customers who haven't yet even bought the first time.

The most profitable phrase in the history of retail marketing has been a McDonald's staple for decades: "Would you like fries with that?"

Too often dismissed as "bonus" sales, the up-sale is nothing of the sort! In most cases, the up-sale is as close as you are ever going to get to pure profit. And profit—not sales—my friend is the only way you stay in business.

Think about it this way: the revenue you generate from every traditional sale you make is balanced against the hard costs of running your business. Subtract the cost of your employees, your power, rent, marketing, debt service, cost of goods, and every little expense that makes up your monthly "nut." The up-sale has already taken into account those costs as well as the customer acquisition costs (what it costs you to get that customer to buy from you for the first time). Anything else you sell them, after the initial order and while you have their attention, is pure profit—minus the cost of goods.

Think of it this way: *Sales generate revenues. Up-sales generate profits!* So, from a marketing perspective, the two messages are often very different, as they are designed to achieve two different behaviors.

Phase one (as discussed in Chapter 4) is designed to achieve the behavior that is predictive of the sale, that is, getting them in the door, on the phone, or to the website (GEICO's "15 minutes could save you 15 percent or more on car insurance."). That ultimate sale can generate the revenue needed to pay your bills.

The phase two "up-sale" message is a "But wait, there's more!" before the final check message that is intended to inform the customer of other opportunities they might not have been aware of. Truly effective sales and marketing professionals design these approaches with the customer's welfare in mind. (No, really!)

A "Supersize" for just pennies more really is a better value. Who wouldn't enjoy a delicious dessert? A higher octane gasoline is better for their car (though not by much). A free duplicate item for only the cost of shipping might be appreciated. "Hmm, you know, this kitchen island would look better with granite, and getting two months free for signing a two-year lease actually saves me money."

The "as seen on TV" industry has mastered the up-sale. While watching a football game with my son, a commercial came on with that familiar: "Order today for just three easy payments of $19.95!" But when they also mentioned the inevitable "Order today and get a second set absolutely free, just pay separate shipping," my son commented that the deal was a "rip-off" because clearly the first item should not have cost so much. "They just overcharged the first one so they can give a second one too!" he asserted. Not necessarily.

The fact is that "second set" does cost them less so they can pass it on at a lower price. All of the acquisition costs are rolled up in the first set. There is no doubt that they will make a strong profit on the first, but they are also paying for the TV air time, production costs, voice talent, media buying, office staff, and more. The second one is the up-sell and only has the cost of the item itself to recover. Of course, they are also making you pay separate shipping and ambiguous "handling" charges, but it's easy to see why they make money.

If you break down the pitch, you can see all the tactics (many of which can certainly translate into your marketing strategy!):

1. **Visibility**—The TV pitch is beamed right to you and, with the right verbiage and energy, can grab and keep your attention.
2. **Context**—You get to see the item being used by very happy people in a variety of situations.
3. **Preferability**—It's not merely a description. You actually see how happy people are and how much they love using it.

4. **Benefit**—An integral part of the pitch is to show you how much better your life will be when you buy and use it: "You keep scrubbing and scrubbing . . . there has to be a better way!"

5. **Price**—The price is only $XX. They might even ask, "How much would you expect to pay?" and before you can answer, they tell you what you might expect to pay. Of course, their price is a fraction of that.

6. **Flexibility**—They give you options to eliminate the price objection. You may not have $120, but you can certainly manage four easy payments of $29.99.

7. **Urgency**—You have to order today, or in the next 30 minutes, or the item is limited to the first 50 callers.

8. **Up-sell**—Double the order, or get a bonus one for low or no cost.

9. **Disclaimer (padding)**—Just pay separate shipping and handling. To be clear, this is a dangerous bait and switch that will bite most of us in the butt. If you aspire to some level of customer loyalty, don't play these games. Give them what they want, the way they want it,

and they are far less likely to go on an online rant.

The up-sell can also take much more subtle forms. In my business, we might suggest to my speaking clients that they tap an "education" budget to purchase a discounted copy of one of my books for each of their members. Everyone wins. They appreciate the creative approach to funding and also get credit for adding value to the audience. The audience/participants appreciate getting a free book (alright, let's call it what it really is: a souvenir) to take with them, and a reminder of the value they received at the meeting or conference. Oh, and I sell more books.

If done aggressively and deceptively, though, you gain a reputation for soaking your customers. Buying additional insurance at the car rental counter is unnecessary and purchasing extended warranties at Best Buy and others are much better deals for them than for you. But approached with a "value-added" mindset, with evocative and persuasive language, customers win and your profits soar.

The up-sell "offenders" piss off their customers to such an extent that they create visible and audible hostility. Often it's a bait-and-switch tactic that lures customers in with a too-good-to-be-true offer, only to be told that what you really want costs more, or you're simply steered toward a more expensive option. The worst of the worst are the airlines. I can see your collective heads nodding in unison.

I do understand the financial pressures facing this volatile industry, but the miserable experience of flying in the 21st century is only being exacerbated by ludicrous new charges and reduced services. The bait is the ultra-low fares. The up-sell is not really an up-sell. It's the switch. We aren't getting "good" and being charged for "better." We are getting ridiculously little and getting charged for what used to be part of the deal: luggage, carry-ons, and a beverage—you know, the basics.

Pity the strained-smiled and overly rehearsed airline representative who attempts to convince us that charging extra for checked bags, carry-on bags, pillows, exit row seats, snacks, priority seating, two wings, pilots, toilet paper, and more is for our benefit. "Why charge everyone for things they don't use?" they inquire incredulously. Of course, only a fraction of flyers fit the narrow criteria.

The lesson for you is that charging extra for basic amenities is not an up-sell. It is abusing the loyalty of your customers or potential customers. Unhappy customers share their unhappiness—with millions.

Probably the most head-scratching offense of the airline industry is how they treat their best customers: the frequent fliers. Let's back up and look at this from a broader perspective. The much touted "80/20" rule has been proven both generally accurate and widely applicable. Essentially, 20 percent of your customers will provide 80 percent of your profits. (Conversely, 20 percent of your customers will provide 80 percent of your problems.)

One of the basic tenants of business is to concentrate on and cater to your core audience. They are the easiest to convince because they need what you are selling. They have the most money, are closest to you, and are most likely to return again and again. Rule #1 in customer service is: don't piss off your best customers! The airlines, in their never-ending quest to become and remain profitable, have been chipping away on the perks offered, increasing the miles and "legs" needed to achieve status, and increasing miles needed for award travel.

Please don't dismiss this as a "First World problem" and the whining of a frequent flier. "Oh, poor, elite flier with their first class seats and full meals on board." This is about profit and perception—and the two are inextricably linked. The lesson applies to your business as well.

When our customers have options from whom to buy (and they always have choices) and when we anger our best customers, we limit our success. When given the chance, they simply leave for greener pastures or kinder ones. Earning them back is a huge challenge. Remember, it's always easier to form an impression than to change one. It's easier to keep a customer than to acquire or convert one.

What does this have to do with up-selling? Up-selling is effective only when the original purchase is considered fair and the additional purchase is looked at as a bonus in some way. It is not supposed to be getting you back to where you thought you should have been in the first place. You want your customers to feel as if they got something more than they had planned for or expected. Taking it away and then selling part of it back to them simply makes your best clients fume.

Requiring minimum purchases, minimum balances, a certain number of flights, deposits, and so on, are often justifiable as long as your best customers get the best deal. And though you don't want to anger anyone, being a less-than-good choice for your worst customers is not always a bad thing.

The little secret of the banking industry is that they make no money on their bottom-tier clients.

Although some may feel like they are being socked for fees on low account balances and ATM use, the truth is that they lose money on low balance accounts. Though they are hoping your business with them will grow, they are less concerned with frustrating low-end account holders as they are with thrilling their top clients. Smart.

Enticing customers with additional up-sell options have built entire aftermarket industries. And though Harley Davidson is often recognized for their fanatical fan base who meet up, "trick out" their bikes, and sport the attire, the reigning king of the aftermarket, up-sell ecosystem is Jeep.

The Jeep enthusiast world is built on the bigger, better, more rugged, more prepared, zombie-apocalypse-ready, on-road, off-road, jacked-up, tricked-out, doors-off, top-off, beach-going, rock-climbing, laid back, and adrenaline junkie options available to all who drive a Jeep. Interestingly, most of the aftermarket options aren't made by Jeep, but by others who have joined the Jeep ecosystem.

Not only has a multi-billion dollar industry been built on the options available to build onto the Jeep JK (Wrangler models), but the physical models are built by Jeep (Chrysler) with holes, connectors, and access to the structure, assuming that aftermarket options will be added. It's not that up-sell options are merely available, they are expected!

Jeep Wrangler models are built with pre-drilled holes and fixtures that can attach new bumpers, lights, foot pegs, soft tops, jacks, winches, reflectors, handles, foot rails, and more. There are spaces for gas cans, locking safe spaces, options for new seats, bigger tires, and body modifications. For Jeep and its aftermarket partners, up-selling is not a bonus, it's an integral part of the business model of the industry and lifestyle brand of its aficionados. You have never owned a Jeep? I do, and as the famous ad campaign asserts: "It's a Jeep thing. You wouldn't understand."

The best up-sells are the ones that you really want to complete the purchase. A meal at McDonald's is not really complete without french fries. An auto insurance policy would not be worth as much to you without emergency roadside assistance; all-you-can-eat restaurants ask if you want to purchase a drink as well; and an automatic car wash is a nice, but the car is not going to be ready to drive without the small upgrade that includes the hot air blow dry.

Along the same lines of the "up-sell as personalization" business model is Build-a-Bear, American Girl dolls, and even many new car models.

Have you ever ordered anything from 1800Flowers.com or Vermont Teddy Bears? It's virtually impossible to check out! Pop-ups, pop-unders, redirects, and more give you countless options to add Teddy bears, chocolates, balloons, and gift cards among other things. Once again, delivered flowers are a commodity and the Internet has driven the margins out of them. The flowers cover the cost, but the up-sell on chocolate, balloons, vases, expedited delivery, and so on drive their profits.

The same model has driven the growth with domain and Web juggernaut GoDaddy.com, print behemoth Vistaprint, and others. Once again, checking out online can take you twice as long as it did to make your actual selection. It may be annoying to encounter, but it works. Even when you call to place an order from a late night television ad for an "As seen on TV" product, be ready for a much longer call than you anticipate. The key, again, is to offer upgrades that are appreciated.

The "do-it-yourself" up-sell would include Pinkberry, Mensches, Yogurtini, or the vast array of make-your-own frozen yogurt shops. Instead of the hard sell, they lay out all the options and you choose how much you want and are willing to pay for. This is very different from the all-you-can-eat restaurant, because with frozen yogurt you are paying by weight. The up-sell options are certainly tantalizing, but completely up to you.

Again, marketing is most effective when you have something interesting to promote. Up-selling gives you more to offer and more to talk about.

The close cousin to the up-sell is the "enhanced model." Though many are reluctant to continue offering the older model when the newest one is released, the truth is that you are missing a golden opportunity to maximize the market. There are always those that will want and be willing to pay for the latest and greatest, whereas others will be fine with the current "old" model.

Logic might suggest that if you can make the old model obsolete, everyone will be forced to purchase the newest one and that will drive additional sales. The truth is that some people will simply bristle at the prospect of having to replace a perfectly good product.

Every time Apple comes out with a new phone, the older model is still available (albeit at a reduced price). They capture those who aspire to what is new and shiny, but also those who cannot afford or simply don't wish to upgrade. The up-sell is simply the better version of what they already have. It's a new product and new revenue, but same customer.

Of course, that newer model will likely need new accessories as the old accessories don't fit the newer model. You didn't think that the lack of backward compatibility was an accident did you?

For many companies, planned obsolescence or a designed shelf life is their lifeblood. In the movie *Joy*, actress Jennifer Lawrence plays famed home shopping entrepreneur Joy Mangano. In a particularly meaningful scene, Joy is presenting her idea for a revolutionary new mop to the president of a mop company and explains that "it's the last mop you will ever need to buy." The company president responds with dismay. Why would he want to sell people their last mop? He wants people to buy lots of mops and to keep buying mops.

Willy Wonka's famed "Everlasting Gobstopper" would never make it to market today. The other companies would buy it and shelve it, or crush Wonka before it crushed the industry.

Most technology companies have a clear idea of the next several iterations of their products with a clear timeline for their release. The "up-sell" is the eventual newest model with incremental enhancements. They have the ability to offer many of those enhancements today, but will hold off for future versions that they can keep up-selling to you.

Another up-sell tactic is the expedited delivery. You can have it faster, but at a cost. Standard shipping might be free, but overnight might cost $20 or more. People will pay for convenience! We want what we want and don't like waiting. We will gladly pay an ATM service fee to save a trip to the bank. We will pay 50 percent more for a grocery item at a 7-Eleven convenience store rather than drive all the way to the grocery store.

Online and on television, the key is to attract and hold attention before asking for the sale. The masters on TV are the fitness infomercials. They are often staged and shot like actual television programs, with interviews, fitness demonstrations, animated explainers, "commercials" within the show itself and, of course, multiple opportunities to buy.

The key for them and for you is to capture and keep the audience's attention. The reigning champ is the fitness company Beach Body, the creators of P90X, Insanity, Brazil Butt Lift, and others. Flipping channels, it's hard not to stop and watch; and once you start watching, it's hard to stop. "I want to look like that," you think to yourself. "Really, just 30 minutes a day?" "Wow, look at that before-and-after picture." "Ya know, that looks fun. I can do that!"

The longer you stay and watch, the more likely you'll buy. It's the same online. Smart companies design their websites to not only differentiate and educate, but to engage the visitor in order to stay longer and dig deeper. Fast food restaurants are joining the premium coffee craze and offering Wi-Fi. Is it to sell more coffee? In part, but mostly it's in an effort to get people to stay longer. If they park their butt at the McCafe and work on their laptop, they will likely get hungry again and keep buying more food.

Car dealerships figured the value of longer engagement a long time ago. You do realize, of course, that when the salesperson goes in the back room to talk to their manager, they're just talking about sports right? Buying a car doesn't really take three to four hours. They just stretch it out so you reluctantly accept the long-negotiated deal rather than starting all over again with another dealership.

Ultimately, smart companies will offer incentives and master the up-sell because it works. It not only helps to ensure your sale, but boosts your profits. To be clear, don't make it a bait-and-switch! It's a bonus, incentive, and reward for being your customer.

The final version of the up-sell is the incentivized purchase. It's the "Wait! There's more! Call now and also receive . . ." They are not actually selling you more; they are giving you more if you agree to purchase now. The added value provided is in exchange for your agreement to move forward with the purchase—now. The retailer knows that the more time passes, the less likely you will be to buy. The fear for you is in missing out on the better price, the extra merchandise, the free consultation, or more.

Marketing to achieve sales is the core of any business success. Businesses often fail because of weak sales exacerbated by poor and ineffective marketing efforts. But for those with a program successful at generating customers, strategic up-sales can bolster the effectiveness of your program and drive multiples in your profitability.

Exercise: Up-Sell Opportunities

There is a term in Web development called MVP. It doesn't stand for Most Valuable Player, but for Minimum Viable Product. To put it simply, many robust e-commerce or membership websites are very complicated and can be very expensive to develop. To save money, many sites are built with just the minimum functionality necessary to make it work from the outset and look great. The additional "bells and whistles" come later when the financial resources are available to add them.

Think of your business offerings in the same way. Is there a base product or service that you can offer with a clear value at the outset, but is a more palatable sale based on a more affordable price?

List all the products or services you offer on a sheet of paper. Now, see if you can deconstruct some of them into multiple parts, with a base-level offering that would still work, or be of value, even without the enhancements. Can you do it? More importantly, could you sell it?

Place a cost of providing it next to the item and then the price you would need to sell it for to make a profit. Then list all of the enhancements you could bolster it with and what you think you could reasonably expect to sell it for. Is there also a way to bundle some of the extras at a reasonable price point?

There will undoubtedly be items and services you offer where this approach will never work. Even in those cases, the value is in the exercise.

When you look at your value propositions in creative new ways, you not only find alternative ways to provide and price things, but potentially discover new ways to rethink meeting customer needs. And being better at addressing customer needs gives you a competitive advantage.

CHAPTER 6

Making and Keeping Your Brand Promise

The biggest lost revenue for your business is prospective customers and clients that you never heard from. They drove by your location, but never came in. They saw an ad, but never called. They went to your website and then clicked away. Worst of all, you don't know who they are, how many of them there are, or how much money you lost.

And what of those who bought from you one time, but never returned? They came in and left. They ate at your restaurant, but never came back. Was it the food, the bathroom, the service, the price, the quality, the location? What? You don't know why? If you are going to grow, you have to know!

So much of success today comes down to the making and keeping of your "brand promise." It's a term that is thrown around quite a bit, but essentially it's an alignment between what you claim, what they expect, and what you deliver. A good choice is a safe choice and promises are meant to be kept. It is just as true in your personal relationships; when you don't keep your promises, people learn that they cannot trust you. If people cannot trust your business to deliver what you say you will, they will flee in droves to your competitors. And trust is hard to earn back. Yes, this is marketing. Everything is marketing.

When you see a sign on a building that says "Under New Management," what they're acknowledging is that you likely had a bad experience with the previous regime. "Try us now! We are waaaaay better!" the sign is meant to convey. Yikes. We all know that it's easier to form an impression than to change one. Do you ever notice that there is a seemingly endless stream of business failures in the same location and that no matter what business goes into that same high-profile location, they don't last very long?

"That building must be cursed!" we say. Well, they are cursed with the ghost of poor management and broken brand promises.

To the consternation of corporate executives, billion dollar brands can be tarnished by the actions of a few individuals in a single location. The Internet has allowed historically private indiscretions to become fodder for the masses. An idiot teenager might have thrown random items into the deep fryer after hours at a fast food joint to the delight of a few fellow workers. Today, that act becomes the viral delight for millions, and the bane of shareholders and franchisees.

"One pep! One cheese!" the disheveled young man shouts to the workers in the back. Five young employees are standing in the kitchen of a Denver area Little Caesars Pizza, wrestling and texting on their cell phones. One of them peels off from the group and begins making two pizzas. Meanwhile, 13 frustrated customers are crammed into the small front area impatiently waiting for orders to make it through the conveyor belt pizza oven, with a line of six more customers out the door. The "Hot and Ready" pizzas promised in their commercials and posters adorning the window are nowhere to be found in the empty warming cases visible to the customers.

With my frustration building, I motion to a young woman standing in the back by the pizza oven, who is likely only a year or two older than the other 16-year-old "workers." "Can I help you," she inquires.

"Why are they making the pizzas to order?" I ask. "There is a huge mob of frustrated customers here. You guys promote that the pizzas are 'Hot and Ready.' I would guess that almost everyone here expected to just grab and go."

"Oh, in the evening, we don't make them ahead of time," she explains. "We want to make sure we don't have any wasted pizzas at the end of the night." By the way, it was only 6:30 p.m. on a Tuesday evening.

My colleague Mark Sanborn calls this "Stepping over dollars to pick up dimes." They might save $5 in food costs by not having a few leftover pizzas at the end of the night, but will lose hundreds of dollars or more from once loyal customers who will think twice about stopping into Little Caesars. This location is no longer a safe choice for those busy parents who stood waiting for far too long.

This isn't a rant about having to wait for a pizza; it's a fundamental lesson about brand promise. In the case of Little Caesars, they started with their first location in 1959, but really burst onto the national scene in the mid 1970s with the

"Pizza Pizza" brand promise. It was two-for-one at a great price. Love it! They have grown into the largest carry out pizza chain in the world.

Today, it's the "Hot and Fresh" promise that is their differentiator. Executed effectively and consistently, it is a brilliant, bankable, and competitive advantage. Why buy from Little Caesars? Because you can save time by just stopping in on the way home and grabbing an affordable, recently cooked pepperoni or cheese pizza from their warming case and go. You don't have to wait. It's "Hot and Ready!"

But Little Caesars failed. If I am running late in the future, I will not trust them to get me in and out fast. They made a promise and then failed to deliver on that promise—intentionally! I really like Little Caesars and love the value proposition, but I will never trust the location near my home to do what they say they will. I will go elsewhere. I assume others there that night, and on other nights, felt the same.

What is your brand promise? Are you living up to it day in and day out? It's important to know that when you make your offer conditional, or change the rules at your liking, the promise is no longer a promise. It is merely a guideline. Translation: you are inconsistent, unpredictable, and no longer a safe choice. Fail!

Volkswagen's broken promises go beyond mere marketing, but to the core of who they purport to be and even potentially into the realm of criminality. One of the attractive benefits of owning a Volkswagen is their great fuel efficiency. But they cheated on the tests by installing software to fool the testing equipment and, in turn, have put their owners in a position of unknowingly and illegally cheating on their emissions tests. And though the "workaround" is purportedly only on their dirtier diesel models, the brand is tarnished forever. Some might trust them in the future, but millions of others won't. They don't really have to trust them or give them a chance in the future. As is true in any competitive environment, there are plenty of other options for us to place out trust. Volkswagen blew it. It's time to move on.

It's crazy that people think they can get away with things in today's marketplace. Everyone has a cell phone to record indiscretions. Employees can copy things on a thumb drive and there are budding Edward Snowdens everywhere. Don't cheat. Don't break promises. We will always find out eventually.

And don't quibble with me about whether you are really promising something if you say you offer it. "There are always exceptions," my client says to me. "People understand that."

No they don't. They understand floods. They understand a city-wide power outage. They even understand a dock workers strike that prevents goods from being offloaded at the port, but they don't understand traffic problems, employee issues, poor management, and excuses. Don't say you are going to do something if you aren't confident you are going to be able to follow through. Don't think for a minute that this is not a big deal. It is!

If a restaurant promotes entertainment on Friday and Saturday nights, but occasionally doesn't have it, we can't make weekend plans with you. You are a risk. If you order flowers for Valentine's Day for your sweetheart and they don't arrive on time, you are in trouble; your relationship is in trouble! More importantly, the floral service is in trouble and your online rants will reach millions. They will lose your future business and will never ever earn it back.

If you tout "friendly service," but don't provide specific service training, or evaluate your staff based on service delivery, then the claim has no meaning. If it's hit or miss, it's a broken promise. You are better off not promising it at all.

Not to sound harsh, but we don't need you! We have plenty of choices. Don't let us down. We likely won't give you a second chance, not because we are mean, but because we are impatient and there are many others who have not let us down. We'd rather try someone new than give a second chance to someone who let us down.

You may be saying to yourself that this seems more like an operations or customer service issue than a marketing issue. Everything that is visible to your customers is a marketing issue. Everything you do in your business—every product or service you develop and offer, every interaction you have with your customers, every word that you write and video that you post—is a reflection on who you are and where you position yourself in the vast sea of marketplace options. You have to make promises to get new clients. You have to keep your promises to keep them coming back.

To compete today, you have to provide more, but don't promote it if you are not going to live up to it. For Little Caesars, their little decision had a big impact on everyone that night—oh, and on everyone reading this as well. D'oh!

Another way to nullify your marketing efforts is to make it hard to do business with you. Difficult-to-navigate websites and "phone menu hell" with too many steps to get what they want makes customers flee. Often, we see internal policies and managers too concerned with being right or winning that they lose sight of why they are in business. I'm not suggesting that the customer is always right, but it's important to accommodate your customers whenever feasibly possible. They pay the bills!

I was with a large group at a casual restaurant in Rotterdam and as we started to push a few tables together, the manager came over and told us that we were not allowed to do so. The place was not crowded and I apologized, but noted that there where 15 of us and we'd like to sit together.

"We can't allow that," he reiterated. "It's just a big hassle to drag the tables back and reset them afterward," he added with a condescending "so sorry" expression on his face.

We left, and their restaurant was still half empty, but it sure looked pretty and neat!

Since when did the staff's convenience take precedent over customer dollars? Are they crazy? Accommodate! Whenever possible, accommodate! Customers are not a pain, they are the reason your staff gets a paycheck. Teach your staff to be accommodating and tell them why.

A bus full of weary teenage football players or a dance troupe pulls up to a restaurant 15 minutes before closing and after the staff has begun to clean up. A retail shop customer purchases 200 items in-store and each one needs to be boxed individually to ship out. A wedding planner books an enormous venue, but a third of the attendees have special dietary restrictions. *So what?*

You are in business to serve, accommodate, and thrill your customers. If you don't, someone else will! You have spent years, if not decades, building your business, don't let your workers cop a poor attitude or show their frustration because they have to work hard. Business is tough! Okay? They are getting paid. You are getting paid. The alternative is far less attractive.

I have a small number of speaker colleagues with a reputation for being a bit of a "Prima Donna." Their contract requires a significant level of accommodation and demands that border on ludicrous. Mine? I list my simple audio/video needs to ensure that my presentation will be effectively received by the audience and confirm the date, time, and location. That's about it. My contract guarantees that I will show up on time and knock it out of the park. That's it. I am the easiest guy to work with—and I work a lot. You want a pre-session call with the company leaders? Sure! You want me to record a short video helping to promote the conference? Absolutely! You'd like an article for your newsletter? What is your deadline?

In today's marketplace, how can you do business any other way?

A gymnastic and dance academy was doing great work with kids. The budding gymnasts and dancers were learning, engaged, and often making great progress. The young instructors were qualified, enthusiastic, and loved working with their kids. Then why was the academy struggling with retention? The kids had a great time, but when it came time to re-enrolling for the next level classes, the parents too often opted out. Why?

I was asked to come in, look at the business, and help diagnose the problems. As I walked through the front doors, the reasons became quickly apparent. Signs littered the premises and in particular, the parents' waiting area, warning of all the things that family members were *not* to do: "No talking to your children during class," "No eating in the viewing area," "We are not a babysitting service. Parents of kids who are not picked up within 10 minutes of class ending will be billed $25," "Missed classes would not be reimbursed without 48 hours notice," and on and on.

The things that made life easier for the staff clearly took precedent over the things that served their customers. The kids were having fun, but the parents certainly were not—and they were the ones writing the checks!

As I began to work with the team, one thing became very clear: none of the wonderful young staff had kids of their own. They loved working with the kids, but they had no clear sense of what the parents were really buying. Sure, they wanted their children to grow and learn, but what they really loved was seeing their children proud of themselves. Watching them learn a new skill, overcome fear, and grow in self-confidence was what they were really paying for. Being able to hang with the other moms and dads and enjoy a snack and a beverage while watching their kids is what made the hour (or hours) go by quicker. But with the numerous restrictions intended to keep the kids safe and the place clean, they were being denied what they were really paying for—a positive experience for themselves and their children.

After shining a light on the buyer's (parent's) motivation and the financial ramifications of the loss of repeat business, they made dramatic changes to their policies. The solutions: Snacks were allowed everywhere except on the gym floor. The end of day vacuuming by the staff was just the price they paid for selling popcorn, pizza, and more. The blunt signage came down, and more importantly, the last five minutes of every class became a mini-recital, where the little cherubs got to show off for mom or dad the new skills they had learned. The kids were excited, the parents beamed, and re-enrollment soared.

A new category of "ultra-cheap" airlines have carved out a dubious niche for unsuspecting travelers. The promise is for very low prices, but only if you plan a very short trip and don't need your stuff like a normal human.

I was checking in for a flight from Singapore to Manila and as I handed my second suitcase to the gentleman at the Tiger Air check-in, a concerned look came over his face.

"Sir, the first suitcase is free, but the second one is going to be very expensive."

"How much will it be?" I asked.

"Based on the weight," he said, "it will be $525 U.S. dollars."

"Are you serious?!" I asked, incredulously. "I only paid $145 for the flight."

Tiger Air, Spirit, Frontier, and the other "low-cost" airlines have created a model that will work financially, for now at least, but the brand loyalty, if it ever existed, is doomed. The second that an alternative is available, their customers will flee in droves. Attempting to retool their value proposition at that point will be nearly impossible because the festering hostility will be so hard to overcome. Once abused by a company, we rarely give them second chances.

Here's where their thinking is flawed: in a static economic model, there is an assumed "cause-and-effect" relationship—that is, charge more money and you make more money. Charge less money and you will get more customers. Raise taxes and you collect more in taxes.

But in a dynamic economic model, human attitudes and behaviors are taken into account in the purchasing behavior assumptions. You can charge less, but if they get far less, people will become dissatisfied. Charge more and they will look for lower-priced alternatives. Anger your customers and they will search for any and every opportunity to avoid doing business with you.

With Tiger Air, I was duped into opting for a low price ticket, but then assaulted with an outrageous charge. With a departing flight to catch, it was easier and cheaper to simply grab a few essential items, leave my suitcase, donate its contents to a local orphanage, and buy new clothes at my next stop than to pay $525 to check it.

I fell for the bait-and-switch—once. If they had charged a reasonably high but acceptable fee, I would have begrudgingly paid it and likely flown with them again, albeit smarter next time. They would then get ongoing revenue from me when I travel through Asia Pacific. As it is now, they didn't get the $525 and will also never get another penny from me. Granted, I may not be their target market, with only a few Asian trips per year, but my money spends as good as anyone else's. Just sayin'.

Today, calls are rarely answered by real people and we spend frustrating minutes caught in "call-menu-hell." ("If you are bleeding profusely from an abdominal wound, press 3.") Do-it-yourself grocery store scanners too often fail to work properly and you have to wait for a "real person" to help you check out. This isn't a rant about bad service. It's an opportunity in the making! As business becomes more and more impersonal, opportunities emerge for you to standout by re-engaging.

When famed entrepreneur Nido Qubein took over as Chancellor of sleepy, southern, High Point University in North Carolina, he brought a unique business mindset to stoic, traditional academia. On one of his first days at the helm, he gathered his staff, told everyone to grab a clipboard and, together, they walked the campus.

He wanted to know what worked and what didn't. He asked why certain things were done the way they were and challenged both long standing tradition and conventional wisdom. When he pointed to a long patch of grass that was worn from foot traffic, a staffer acknowledged, "That is where the students cut across the grass to get to the other building."

"Well, if that's where they want to walk," Qubein declared, "then pave it for them!"

Any parent of a student nearing the end of high school knows that the mail box will soon be overflowing with brochures and letters from colleges trying to recruit their student. Especially for those with good grades and strong test scores, the onslaught can be overwhelming. Colleges know that they have to "market" to get the best kids because the best kids are in demand and have numerous options.

High Point University runs like a business. They know their customers are not just the prospective students, but Mom and Dad. The marketing materials they send will blow away most companies in America. They make the student feel wanted, appreciated, and "selected."

Although High Point University has an impressive number of scholarships available for the best students (they are competing against the best colleges), they have one requirement: before any funds will be offered, you have to visit the campus.

High Point University is very clear on the one behavior that is predictive of success—getting a student and their parents on the campus. Just as GEICO wants 15 minutes and a car dealership offers a test drive and Panda Express offers a sample of Orange Chicken, High Point knows that once you visit, you will be overwhelmed by the amount of thought that has gone into designing this stunning university campus.

For those unfamiliar with High Point University, imagine if you combined Harvard, Nordstrom, and the Ritz Carlton. This mash-up would result in High Point University. The grounds are immaculate and the facilities are traditional southern in architecture, but are state of the art in amenities. The student center features a farmer's market, sports bar, and movie theater with stadium seating. In fact, there is so much to do and be involved in that over 95 percent of students live on campus.

With the countless upgrades, additions, and revisions enacted from billions of dollars raised, the last 10 years has seen a transformation that now has High Point University enjoying a Number 1 ranking from *U.S. News & World Report* as the best college in the south and the nearly 5,000 students benefiting from the "Most Spoiled College in America" designation from *USA Today*. And as the college expands, builds new facilities and astonishing amenities for their students, large signs with artistic renderings of the new buildings reminds supporters of "Promises Kept!"

What Nido Qubein has really done is created an extraordinary brand. The vision was for a university that is impossible to ignore, run and marketed as a dynamic business with products and services, tangible deliverables, customers they must compete for, and stakeholders that must be kept engaged. Diligence has ensured the growing structure supports the vision and the result has been a university like no other.

What? You haven't heard about High Point University? Oh, you will. (Better yet, if you have a high school student, Google it!)

IKEA is famous for looking at the traditional retailer model and re-thinking the customer experience. They challenged the model and built a new kind of store. From store flow and layout to the items themselves, IKEA has taken a unique approach to how we buy, transport, assemble, and even display their products in our home.

At most stores, they make you abandon your shopping cart to go down the escalator, or just wait for an elevator. If the shopping cart is full, you have to take the items out and carry them or use the hard-to-find elevator. IKEA created a moving walkway escalator ramp, and so that the carts don't roll away down the ramp, the wheels are magnetic. They grab hold and lock the shopping cart into place as soon as you get on the ramp. Brilliant!

This isn't just about reinventing your business, sparking innovation, or staying ahead of the curve. This is a more fundamental examination of every single "touchpoint" of your business and asking: "Is that the way it needs to be done? Where do we fall short, or can we do better than the competition on this?"

Do you ever get frustrated with a business and ask yourself: "Do these guys ever try to call their own company? Why would anyone design a system that is so maddening for their customers?" The problem for most is that they do go through the process of shopping themselves or calling their number, but they are looking through the eyes of an employee or owner with a base-level of knowledge of how it's supposed to work correctly. Then they gauge their impressions and experience based on the company standard. The problem is that your customers don't have any idea of the back office, inner workings, or the company standard! They just know that they are confused, frustrated, or inconvenienced.

Companies that "secret-shop" themselves fall into this trap. Although it is important to ensure that your staff is behaving according to your training when management is not around, customers have no idea about what was trained. Outside impressions can be very valuable, particularly when they represent your prime demographic. Have others report their experience or hire a reputable secret shopping service. You may be surprised at what you find.

We see this dynamic with content-rich websites. Too often, the site is so jam-packed with information that you can't figure out where to find what you want. The creators of the site and staff know where to click and find the information because they work with it every day, but they aren't going to be with you each time to explain it.

If they were sitting right next to you, they could tell you to: "Go to the Home page and then go to the About tab and then scroll down, then click on Team and then scroll down to find the department that you want. Good. Now click Department, then scroll to find the person you want. Click on them, then scroll to the bottom and click on Contact and if you don't want to fill out the contact form, you can go back up to the Home button, click on that, then go to the far right and click on Corporate. Find the office you want and ignore the contact form, but scroll all the way to the bottom to can find the phone number." Ugh!

Then, when you finally get a phone number and call, you are greeted with "Listen closely, as our options have changed." You figure you might as well make some popcorn 'cause this is going to be awhile.

Why do we all groan and roll our eyes at scenarios like this? *Because they are true!* They happen all the time. Do you not see how ludicrous this is? Is this you?

What is the most visited Webpage in the world? Of course, it's Google. What can Google teach us about simplicity, ease of use, and customer experience online? Can you imagine how difficult it was for Google to say "no" to all the things they could have put on their home page? Thousands of very proud and capable employees have "taken one for the team" by not showcasing their countless great ideas. The home page is simple and effective. It's sparse and remarkably intuitive.

Secret shop yourself. Call your company and try doing what you ask your customers and prospects to do. Order a product from your own company and see how long it takes to go through the process and for items to arrive. See how long you are placed on hold during peak times.

There is no eloquent way to say this: You are killing yourself if your customer experience sucks.

One of the many challenges with corporate America is that the people responsible for marketing are not in the room when customer-centric decisions are being made. Rarely are internal issues strictly internal. Most have an external impact.

I not only speak to audiences of business owners and CEOs, I also offer insights on competitive advantages to C-level professionals in operations, human resources, logistics, finance, research and development, and more. Why would someone with no marketing responsibility in their organization care about marketing? Because marketing is not a department. This is not to suggest that you don't have a marketing department; rather, it's the recognition that virtually everything done within your organization has an impact on how you are perceived in your marketplace.

When service is cut to save dollars, customers notice. When new product development and creativity stagnates, you lose competitive advantage. When logistics hits a snag, then products arrive late and customers are frustrated. When you fail to attract and develop top talent, then your competitors grab them and put them to work against you.

Keep in mind that the role of marketing is not "spin." It's not about clever messaging to mask deficiencies in your operation. Marketing is not about "putting lipstick on a pig"! Marketing is sharing with your audiences who you are, what you do really well, and why they should buy from you, now.

Don't waste dollars asking prospects to try you out if you are not really great. You are essentially asking: "What do you think?" And if the answer is "Meh," or worse yet, frustration, you've just wasted your money. It's much easier to form an impression than to change one. If you deliver a sub-standard product, experience, exchange, or service, you've got a long road ahead to change that person's mind. Remember, dissatisfied customers rarely complain. They just don't come back. Getting them back after they've left is an exercise in futility. You're better off going after a new prospect.

Step back, examine your business, fix your issues, improve your process, and train your people. Re-evaluate long standing assumptions. Survey your customers. Why do they like you? Why did they leave you?

There is a lost art in business today: it is the exit interview. Although many have done them, too many HR staffers in large organizations simply go through the motions because it's a part of their established process, without really understanding why they are doing them. Even in those cases, I wonder if anyone reviews or acts on the information revealed.

The information gathered in a well-executed exit interview can be a gold mine for business, but too few have the courage to conduct them. Why? Because they are uncomfortable! How many times did you meet with a love interest over coffee soon after a breakup, sit down with a pen and paper, and ask: "Let's talk about why you are leaving me. So, what do you think I did well in this relationship and where did I fall short?" Yuck!

If you really want to know what is going on in your business, especially when you are not there, ask the employees who leave you. You can certainly learn something from the ones you fire, but the valuable information comes from good people who opt out. Remember that quality employees have options; the bad ones don't. Dissatisfied, but talented, people leave for greener pastures. If you ask them to share with you why, many will actually tell you. Don't dismiss their words.

Go beyond the standard questions and ask: "What do you wish you would have known before you accepted this job? Where do you think we didn't live up to our claims? If you could wave a magic wand, what are three things you would change about this company? What could we have done differently to have kept you? What are others feeling about their job and this company? What do you think is happening that's hurting morale, customer loyalty, sales, retention, and innovation?"

Of course, there are a myriad of reasons that people leave and we are often happy that they did, but use a reasonable filter when reviewing these responses while avoiding the temptation to dismiss anything outright. Your team possesses a wealth of insights as they are on the front lines every day. Departing staffers often have nothing to lose and will often tell you what others won't. Don't ignore this important opportunity. And though you can't force participation, you can certainly incentivize it. The issues they reveal are often visible to your customers. You can't address them if you are not aware of them.

Another significant problem in business is that, too often, the structure doesn't support the vision. You may aspire to be a dynamic company with cool products and fantastic service, but if your primary interface is arduous, customers will flee. You can claim that "your people make the difference," but without a differentiating screening mechanism, specific training, and a reinforced service culture, your words are meaningless. Worse yet for those that fail to meet the claimed standard, you have broken your brand promise. Once again, in a competitive marketplace, broken promises are not easily forgiven.

Some in large organizations have adopted the tactic often referred to as Management by Walking Around (MBWA). However, there is only so much that can be accomplished through mere internal visibility. The popular television program *Undercover Boss* has taught company leaders to not assume that they know what happens on the front lines of their own businesses. It is only through real world scenarios and personal interactions that you can know what your customers and prospects experience.

You can achieve competitive advantage and an enviable reputation by being remarkably easy to do business with. Think beyond the basic issues of customer service and product mix and look at the minutia. You can drive dollars from details! In the best of cases, not only will you stem the tide of lost business by addressing deficiencies, but you might, in turn, actually create additional opportunities through your systematic introspection and self-examination.

Unfortunately, during challenging economic times, the bean counters will often win the war, while sales and marketing are left with the unenviable task of selling the diminished brand and dubious value proposition.

"Thin, hard, plastic airplane seats will allow for more passengers," the airline cost-cutters say. Voice mail will eliminate costly staffers. Offshore customer support employees (with poor English skills) are much more affordable. Charging for extra ketchup packets at the drive-through will add up to big revenue over time. Dumb!

I am not ranting about the loss of service, connection, amenities, and respect. I am pointing out where new opportunities exist by not being like those companies. Don't just fix what is broken or is less than ideal at your business, but look at what people hate about your industry and competitors and offer better alternatives in your business model. Sometimes, the biggest opportunity to gain a competitive advantage is by offering what your competitors no longer do.

Remember, the best restaurant experience in the world will be nullified by a dirty restroom.

Grab your magnifying glass and get your operations and delivery in tip-top shape before you ask others what they think.

Exercise: Why Do We Do It That Way? Why Do We Say "No"?

Assertions like "That's the way we do things here" can be a powerful reaffirmation of a strong company culture, or it can be a default response demonstrating ingrained complacency. Regardless, it's often easier to simply fall back on policy rather than invest the time and effort into challenging our assumptions and improving our systems.

Everything we do in our business is based on a decision made at some point by somebody. Whether or not the same conditions exist today that led to that decision is a different matter altogether. Do you have a process in place to periodically revisit policies, procedures, behaviors, staff interactions, and customer expectations?

Let's look at your interactions with your customers or clients: To what questions do your employees say "no" to when dealing with customers? Is it in regard to payment options, return policy, delivery schedules, direct access to company leadership, food or drink on the premises, or customer support? Are we saying "no" out of convenience or habit when there is a reasonable option for saying "yes"?

Gather your team together and be sure to include front line staff who have direct customer or client contact. Take out a piece of paper and work together to brainstorm both common and challenging interactions. These scenarios of customer conversations might occur in person, by e-mail, or over the phone. Write down as many questions that a customer has asked or might ask that you can think of. Which of those requests or questions do you say "no" to?

Ask the team: "Why do we say 'no'? Is it for our convenience? Is it because it would cost us money or take too much time away from our normal activities?" The more profound question to ask your team is: "Is there a way we can say 'yes'? Would finding a way to say 'yes' increase customer loyalty, differentiate us from competitors, and help us to become a better choice?"

CHAPTER 7

Promote the Hell Out of Your Business!

It has been said that doing business without promotion is like winking at someone in the dark. You know what you are doing, but nobody else does!

I have a confession to make: I don't utilize all of the strategies and tactics I teach from the stage and profess in my books. It's not that I don't believe in what I teach, I most certainly do! It's just that I don't have the time or resources to do everything. No one does. I don't utilize all of the social media options available. I don't blog as much as I should. My website isn't updated frequently enough and

I sometimes fail to capture contact information from prospective customers and clients.

But don't use the excuse of being overwhelmed to not do more than you are currently doing to market and promote your business. At the very least, determine the most appropriate and effective tactics and embrace those. When time and resources allow for more, do more.

Too many in business have discarded traditional media in favor of the new strategies and tactics of social media, video, and other Internet resources. It would be a mistake to disregard the older methodologies merely because so many have moved on. An integrated marketing approach can offer enhanced results that narrow ones cannot.

One of the more interesting reasons that traditional media can be a valuable component in your marketing arsenal is that it's actually becoming more effective in recent years. As people flee traditional avenues, those avenues become far less crowded. Translation: fewer competitors mean more eyes and ears for your message!

Although newspaper advertising declines have mirrored the drastic drop in readership, there is still a huge value in small, local newspapers. Where else can local readers learn about developments in their community, scores from the local school teams, craft fairs, fundraising events, recreation schedules, and more? The eyes are still there and the prices have dropped, which means more bang for your advertising dollars.

The other benefit to local newspapers (and their online partners) is that they are dying for stories to write! Puff pieces, business profiles, and local event coverage that would never have made it into a large metropolitan newspaper are grist for the mill for the neighbor rags (and I use the term "rag" with much affection).

Along the same lines, radio can still be a great venue for delivering your message to a very targeted audience. The good news is that they are happy to do the research for you, broken down into 15-minute day-parts. The better news is that you get to control the content and the message. You can write the script for the recorded message as well as the live read from the on-air personality.

The most important thing to remember, as is true with all campaigns, is that you have to constantly evaluate the effectiveness of the dollars spent. Is the message working? Is the venue effective? Did I give it enough time to truly gauge the response and return on investment?

Remember that the advertising salespeople are paid on commission and will do everything they can to sell you more and lock you into long-term contracts. Do short tests before you commit long term.

The other traditional media that is seeing a resurgence is direct mail and even door hangars. Direct mail lost much of its luster because of the high cost of printing and the rising cost of mailing. Worse still was that your flyer was often lost in a large stack of junk mail received by prospects and you would be lucky to receive the industry standard 4 percent response rate.

The good news for you is that most in business believed those who asserted that e-mail could reach the same people at a fraction of the cost. Though the reach is certainly cheap, the effectiveness of e-mail blasts is minimal at best. We still have junk mail; there is just more of it and it's just now on our computers.

Our traditional mailbox is now largely empty, except for the ever-present bills and occasional supermarket adds and catalogues. Direct mail is once again attractive because you no longer get lost among the junk mail that is a fraction of what it was a decade ago.

If your customers are within a 1–3 mile radius, hang a well-designed piece on their doorknob, pass out coupons at neighboring businesses, or forge a reciprocal arrangement with a local business who shares the same audience.

Much of my success as a professional speaker can be directly attributed to traditional methods of marketing and sales. My staff writes countless letters and e-mail pitches to meeting planners. We mail brochures and other marketing pieces. We pick up the phone and follow up on pitches and even occasionally set up a trade show booth at a conference to pitch my speaking and sign books. Of course, I have a significant social media presence with top YouTube rankings and numerous posts, but my traditional marketing approaches are a crucial element to my work.

Some of the biggest growth in both reach and opportunities for businesses today is with content marketing. From writing articles and posting blogs to forwarding relevant content of others, content marketing has become a cash cow for some while remaining enigmatic for others.

In yesteryear, we spent a great deal of time and effort trying to persuade reporters and editors to write a story about us or about our business. Getting that coveted story in the newspaper was considered valuable "free advertising" and meant that you had arrived. The tradeoff was that, although there was a measure of influence as to what was being written, there was no control. We pitched the story and rolled the dice.

Today, you don't need others to decide if your story is worthy. Just write the story, blog, rant, top 10 list, profile, expose, or essay yourself! The venues for posting such information are vast, and some clearly offer more exposure than others. The value in visibility is tremendous. Content marketing gives you the chance to say what you want, offer your insights and expertise, and educate your market about your content.

Content is also a vital component in bolstering your "find-ability" online. Keywords strategically placed in your titles and articles, as well as backlinks, are crucial to boost your search rankings and are not only important for you, but also make your content attractive to others who benefit by posting your content through their channels. Great content, wisdom, opinions, information, and more are the breadcrumbs spread throughout the world that lead people to your website and your business.

Just Google "Article Submission Sites" and you will find a wealth of places to send articles and content by others. In addition to their posting of your content, they will distribute it to other sites, or others will pull content from them, greatly extending your reach.

The content you create or share through both traditional mechanisms and social media outlets offers you a measure of permanence as well. Though newspapers might get thrown away, the Internet lives on and on. So, don't only share content through your LinkedIn account, Twitter, blogs, and more, also share with others who are looking for content. Guest blogs, newspaper columns, and vast online forums offer a bullhorn for your content.

Be cautious, however, and take a moment to breath before posting rants or content created in anger. The old adage holds true: Don't share anything you wouldn't want your parents to read.

A final note about content marketing (a subject that others have written entire books about): the content itself is key! Information is a dime-a-dozen. Say something new. Add a fresh perspective or a controversial take. Create something easily shared (top 5 or top 10 lists). And as I will continue to repeat throughout this book: "If you want people to be interested, you need to be interesting!"

The virtual 800 lb. gorilla is social media. The growth has been explosive, although the formula for successful business use for many has been elusive. For the eager adopters and the naysayers alike, here is what we know: social media's reach is vast, its influence is pervasive, and the future is unknown.

People will look at the massive landscape of social media and often feel so overwhelmed that they get paralyzed. Even technology natives like those in their teens and 20s who embrace social media don't participate in every online vehicle. In fact, soon after older generations begin to catch on and delve into the same resources, they will often move on to "cooler" pastures. Honestly, even I find it all overwhelming at times, and I teach this stuff! But I know where my audience goes to connect. I know where they seek information and resources and I make certain that I am there—hardcore!

The point is you have no excuse not to promote. There is little point in "following your passion," developing products and services, and building your business if you don't get out there and effectively raise your visibility, promote your business, and deliver your message.

Visibility marketing is to understand how crucial it is to get out of your box, location, warehouse, salon, restaurant, office, and home and reach your customers and prospects *where they are!* The tactics, tools, vehicles, and venues available to us are truly remarkable today. More importantly, your competitors are already there, or will be soon.

Everything else covered in this book is intended to bring you to this moment. We have clarity of our core competency. We understand our marketplace. We acknowledge the attraction of our competitors and what makes them worthy. We recognize the needs and deficiencies in the marketplace. We understand or have created competitive advantage within our business. We have crafted messages that do more than merely inform, but truly persuade and convince our prospective customers and clients that we are a better choice than their other choices. Now, it's time for you to get to work promoting your business, sharing your message, and creating visibility!

Ask yourself: Where are all of the places that my prime prospects receive information? What do they watch? What do they read? Where do they recreate, congregate, dine, connect, and gather? What social media platforms do they frequent? Who are their influencers? Who is their tribe and where do they get their information and affirmation?

These are not rhetorical questions. Grab a cup of coffee (or pour yourself a beer), pull out a pad of paper, and write down answers to each question. And if you have multiple markets or audiences (for example, you might sell to consumers and the government, or you might serve singles and families), then you need to have an answer for each question for each audience. If you have employees, partners, or other team members, make this a group activity. Ask each other these questions. Challenge the answers and your assumptions.

Yes, this will take some time, but why else are you taking the time to read this book? The good news is that most of your competitors will not take the time it takes to dig deep. Most will believe that if they just create great products or service, provide value and great service, then the rest will take care of itself. We both know that isn't true.

Visibility marketing is not just about reaching the right people where they are; you have to do it at the right time, in the right venue, and with a profoundly effective and memorable message.

How often do you see ads for weight loss or fitness products in September or March? Almost never. Why? Because in September, people start putting warmer clothes back on and are less concerned with how their body looks. In March, they've already stopped going to the gym that they bought the membership for in December. If the fitness industry spends money at the wrong time, most of it will be wasted.

You know when the weight loss and fitness marketing barrage takes place: December and January to coincide with New Year's resolutions, and then again in the spring to prepare for bathing suit season. 24-Hour Fitness, NutriSystem, Weight Watchers, and others likely have highly effective fitness and weight loss offerings and brilliantly well-crafted messages, but delivered at the wrong time. It's dollars down the drain.

When do you see commercials for Vermont Teddy Bears, Edible Arrangements, Massage Envy, and Zales popping up on your television screens? Of course it's during the weeks leading up to Valentine's Day. It's a smart strategy—promote during the time of year your core customers are more likely to buy.

Is there a time of year that customers are more likely to buy what you are selling, or can you tailor your message to make them consider you more during that time? Anchor your message and your promotional spending to coincide to that time. You might be thinking that "it's the other times of the year, the slow time, that I need to bolster my sales." That might be true, but the smart money is spent maximizing the times that your prime customers are more likely to buy.

Spring is a great time to push the gift aspect of your products for "Dads and Grads." Mother's Day is great for cards and sweet gifts. Thanksgiving is a perfect time to push home decor as people look to spiff up their home before guests arrive. Fall is prime time for "nesting" as people buy organizers and more to get things put away for winter. Summer is good for backyard items, fall for the winterizing, and so on.

The real opportunity, often, is not for the obvious calendar targeting, but to look at your products and services and see if there is a way to spin the message to make it appear timelier during certain times. Companies that make clear storage bins will often do a limited run during the summer of red and green bins using the same molds and sell them as "Christmas Decoration Bins." Marshmallow makers will add pastel colors for Easter, and candy makers will roll out the "fun size" for Halloween.

A proximity strategy is also important to consider. Though some businesses are truly global, many really do pull from the standard 3–5 mile radius. A tanning salon located in the northern suburb of a major city might have perfectly connected their message and their timing, but if the venue/vehicle is ill-advised, the campaign falls short. If they buy newspaper or television ads covering the entire city, then they're wasting money. Although they may reach many of their targeted prospects, 90 percent of the people they are paying to reach would never drive all the way to their location. It's a great strategy, but the wrong vehicle.

A financial service provider in a major Midwest city had a large firm of advisors. He and his team were the clear market leader and were expanding to the other major city in their state. His team did extensive research and obtained contact information for thousands of high net-worth prospects in that new city. They spent months creating a package of targeted marketing pieces and spent tens of thousands of dollars printing and sending a mass mailing to all of them.

Unfortunately, the printed piece used far too common language and claims that mirrored other firms already in that space, and the letter from the firm principal was far too long. As a kicker, they also included a USB thumb drive in the package loaded with additional material that actually would have proven very valuable to prospects—if the recipients actually plugged it into their computer and viewed the contents. Of course, they didn't.

They didn't get a single response. You can probably guess why. Despite the claims of the advertising specialties salesperson who sold them on the promise of the custom USB drives, people were reluctant (read: scared) to insert the device into their computers for fear of viruses and other malware.

That's tens of thousands of dollars wasted. They had the right strategy, but used the wrong tactic.

To maximize the effectiveness of both the effort and dollars, the "hub and spoke" model is often a powerful approach. Rather than attempting to reach all of your desired targets yourself, employing others to relay the message can be very effective. It's the core of what public relations is all about. Tapping into the networks and reputations of others can bolster your reach and influence. Pitching stories, writing stories, blogs, tweets, and disseminating through others' broadcast audience, mailing lists, social media network, newspaper and blog readers, YouTube subscribers, and more amplifies your reach.

The key is meeting the needs of the "hub" to get them to open access to their "spokes." There is a maxim that, though cynical to be sure, holds true: "When trying to get someone to do something, don't appeal to their better nature. They may not have one. Appeal to their self-interest and you'll get farther."

The marketing partners' hubs have needs. A particular need is for relevant content to keep the lines of communication buzzing. Reporters need daily stories to write. Bloggers need blogs to fill the gaps when they have nothing to share. Tweeters need content to bolster their message and keep their followers engaged.

When asking, however, reciprocity is key! If you are going to ask, you'd better be willing to give. Nobody likes a "taker" and reputations are hard to shake. If you are going to ask others to open up their network, you better be prepared to respond in kind. I am not talking about allowing others to indiscriminately blast your minions with pitches, but partnering with like-minded, non-competing colleagues to provide limited and appropriate content to each other's audience.

If your pizza place longs to reach dozens of kids and their parents who come in and out of the tae kwon do studio four doors down, then offer to put a countertop display promoting their business, if they will do the same for you. Mutual audience + different offering + close proximity = cross-promotional nirvana.

Once again, the best way to potentially out-market your competitors is to create products and services that are more marketable. If you give your team more to talk about, they'll have more to talk about. And then, if you combine products that are truly exceptional, and marry them with out-of-the-box creative and strategic promotion, you will have the opportunity to generate significant buzz.

For example, we live in the age of portable food and drink. It's not just purchasing food and drink on the go, but the actual portability of those items. Sport bottles are cheap and convenient; bottled water is a billion-dollar industry. Meals on the go are readily available at the drive-up window, while grocery stores, convenience stores, sandwich shops, hotdog carts, and coffee spots litter every corner.

So, how do you take a pervasive convenience and make it buzzworthy? The creative geniuses at Hydro Flask took the old-school insulating value proposition of the familiar Thermos container and combined it with the convenience and popularity of the water bottle to create a next generation water bottle and food container that breaks the mold. Of course, we are no longer impressed by "gee whiz" for the sake of "gee whiz." It has to solve a problem not yet adequately addressed by current marketplace offerings, and "new" only goes so far.

The reality of the current generation water bottles and sport bottles is that all they do is hold your liquid and allow them to be taken with you. This is a nice convenience to be sure, but the down side is that they don't keep hot drinks hot and cold drinks cold for very long. The tall, coffee versions of the travel mug do an adequate job and are a step up from traditional, wide-mouth coffee mugs, but the heat retention is measured in minutes, not hours.

The Hydro Flask uses proprietary technology to extend the temperature retention to a profoundly "news worthy" degree. And to demonstrate the insulating value of their new products, they created a little demonstration. Marketing representatives from Hydro Flask sent their drink bottles to writers and reporters from select media outlets that cater to "outdoorsy" and mobile consumers. They sent the drink bottle by regular mail and included a note asking the reporters to hold off on opening the bottle until called.

So, three days after the bottles were mailed, the phone call came in to the reporters who were instructed to open the Hydro Flask container and describe the contents. What did they find? Ice. Three days after being placed in the bottle and shipped across the country through regular delivery mail, the ice remained. Remarkable indeed! They could have sent a brochure to describe the properties of the Hydro Flask, but the reporters were never really going to "get it" until they got it. Get it? Of course, they in turn told their readers and followers. Would a press release have accomplished the same impact? Hardly.

Hub and spoke? Absolutely! The outdoorsy magazines have access to their targeted population. Hydro Flask met their needs by providing a truly newsworthy story about a cool technology that would be of great interest to their readers. They pitched it in a clever way that made the editors stand up and take notice and made a compelling case for the legitimate news value to the magazine's readers. Hydro Flask got others to share their message. The magazines and news outlets fulfilled this mission of providing relevant content to their audience and the target market learned of a cool new resource that would support their lifestyle. Win. Win. Win.

To tap into the audiences and networks of others to broadcast our message, we must meet their needs in some way. You can help colleagues by providing content for their blogs. You can help a reporter look good by giving them a great, legitimate story to cover (not simply free advertising for you). You can reciprocate a positive mention by retweeting someone else's content.

As they say: *the behavior that is recognized and rewarded is the behavior that is repeated!*

What is needed is a well-considered and well-crafted connection between our words and their wants; our platforms and their patterns; our creativity and their consumption; what we want to say, and what they want to hear.

Although this is primarily a strategic book, aligning the tactics is profoundly important. Billions of dollars have been wasted chasing marketing fads, delivering ineffective messages, misaligning data with messaging, and generally just winging it. Visibility marketing is about a shift in mindset and approach toward effectively reaching your customers within the context of a very competitive marketplace.

With that shift in mind, the book would not be complete without an examination of effective tactics to illustrate and implement the strategic advice. Keep in mind that some of the specific social media platforms and tactics in particular might become quickly outdated as the industry shifts constantly. The lessons, however, hold true.

There is a reason that the word visibility has been prevalent throughout the book. Visibility is often the missing link that is predictive of ultimate business success or failure. Today, more than ever, people look before they buy. They search for answers, products, people, companies, services, resources, and more. Of course, people have always searched, but today they search online.

The profound shift in power from the provider to the consumer has been driven by the easy access of information. We don't need to look to providers to educate us. We do it ourselves. The question for you is: When people look, do they find you? And, more importantly, what do they find? My colleague Heather Lutze asked that profound question in her breakout book, *The Findability Formula.* Your prospects are looking. How findable are you?

As much as we'd love for people to flock to our websites, the reality is that most will come to you through some other means. On LinkedIn, for example, with an enhanced membership, you can not only see who has viewed your profile, but you can see how they found you. Perhaps it was through a mobile search, by clicking others like you, or through a referral from a colleague. The path can be indirect, but it often comes down to the breadcrumbs you leave behind.

I received a call from a Los Angeles-based talent agency representative last year telling me that her firm was working with a television producer interested in me as the possible host of a new business turnaround reality program under development for a major cable television network. As I live in the Denver, Colorado area, far from New York or

Los Angeles, I asked where they had learned about me. She said that they found me online.

"I have a number of short business marketing videos online," I told her.

"We know," she responded enthusiastically. "We have been watching them for the past 45 minutes! The producers love you. Where did you come from? Why didn't we know about you?" she demanded, with a smile. in her voice.

In the end, the fit wasn't right, but you can bet I am on their radar for future opportunities. What was the key? *Visibility!* How visible are you across all the avenues that people search for resources?

If you want customers, partners, vendors, prospects, and others to find you, you have to be findable. If you want them to be interested, you have to be interesting. If you want them to interact with you, then you need to be interactive. That sounds basic, but you have to constantly reevaluate how you are being received and stay diligent.

Your greatest challenge in business is most often not your competitors—it's anonymity. If they don't know who you are, they can't buy what you're selling. If they don't remember you, then you are not even in the running. You need to be top-of-mind when prospects are looking to buy. Social media and other online resources can play a big role in staying in front of prospects.

Let's be honest. The vast majority of companies using social media do a terrible job. Most in business just look at it as another venue to replicate what they say in their ads, brochures, or websites. What they choose to post is often just another commercial for their business—except that it's on social media! Bad idea. In yesteryear, we learned to avoid ads by grabbing the remote control and clicking away from television commercials. What do you think people are doing to your self-promotional social media postings? Yep, they're clicking away.

I am often asked what the secret is to getting something to go "viral" online. The response is simple. I tell them: "Just post something that is so interesting that someone would actually want to pass it on to someone else." "No. Really," they say again. "Uh, really!" I respond.

So, what does "interesting" look like to your prospective customers? Certainly, what is interesting is subjective. What captures the attention of one person might differ vastly from another. That said, you should have a pretty good idea of what constitutes a strong customer prospect for your business. They share certain attributes that can be used as the basis for a strong marketing effort.

If your demographic is primarily women and you offer a highly visual array of items, then you'd be crazy not to have a strong presence on Pinterest. And though teens have fled from Facebook in droves, they are all over Instagram, Vine, Snapchat, and others. Business people are connecting though LinkedIn. Twitter connects thought leaders to their minions and Facebook has helped to humanize both people and organizations by providing a venue for sharing the personal side of our multifaceted lives.

Despite the vast number of social media websites vying for your attention and usage, there is still no better resource to communicate, connect, engender, and galvanize support and engagement than video. As of this writing, Google is the top search engine in the world. It may surprise you to learn that the number two search engine is YouTube. When people search, they are not just looking for traditional information. Today they want highly visual examples such as pictures, animations and, of course, video!

As I mentioned earlier, I speak for a living. And although a high Google ranking is always desired, my clients come to me through YouTube. There are few purchases riskier than hiring a well-compensated speaker you've never heard speak.

Audiences will let you know if the speaker hit it out of the park or fell flat and nobody wants to find out after the fact. Video is the virtual "sampling" to professional speakers that before and after pictures are to a plastic surgeon. To make a safe purchasing decision, meeting planners need to see what I do. YouTube is crucial to my business model and a high placement assures me a spot as a speaker to be considered when planning committees meet to pick their conference presenters.

Because of the importance of that online vehicle, I spend my time, money, and creative resources to ensure that I am found when others are searching. When meeting planners look for professional speakers, they look on YouTube. As of this writing, if you search YouTube for the term "Marketing Speaker," I am number one—in the world! When you search "Best Marketing Speaker," once again, I hold the top spot.

To be clear, it doesn't mean I am the best marketing speaker in the world (then again, it doesn't mean that I'm not). What it says is that I have sufficient video content and engagement to earn the top spot—organically! When meeting planners are searching for what I do, at the very least I know that I am being considered.

There is no shortage of resources to show you how to best use social media. In fact, you have only to visit YouTube and search "How to use" any of the social media resources and you will be greeted with a lengthy menu of tutorial options. The real challenge (and opportunity) comes from the quality and relevance of the content that you shared and the strategy behind it.

Too many share content for the sake of volume. I saw a tweet from Del Monte which shared that it was about a month away from harvest time. They encouraged followers to click "Like" to wish the corn "Good Luck." Uhhh . . . "Good luck little corn! You can do it!" Stupid! This is what happens when interns and others are handed the reins and post for the sake of presence and volume and not for beneficial, strategic, and authentic engagement.

Many have invested significant dollars into social media as their primary mechanism for connecting with their audiences. My brilliant speaker colleague Sima Dahl teaches: "Social media does not replace traditional marketing. It amplifies it!" Historically, marketing has been "pushed" out to prospects and customers. When we have something to say, we send it out. It might be through a press release, TV commercial, print ad, flyer, or other means.

Social media provides an interactive marketing vehicle to elicit conversation, feedback, and engagement as long as you follow the rules! Don't sell—share. It is a perfect "hub and spoke" to reach not only our fans and followers, but the followers of our followers.

Despite the original intent of the developers, most social media platforms will illustrate the unpredictable reality of "chaos theory" and find its own path. LinkedIn was envisioned as a database to connect to the people you want to meet through the people you already know. The warm hand-off, the online, trusted introduction was the promise of the early adopters. You could request an introduction and that introduction was welcomed because you both knew the connecter. But what happened? Most professionals don't limit their connection to people they know, but also include people they want to know. So, the trusted introduction has become less trusted and, therefore, less frequent.

LinkedIn today is a search engine for business professionals. It is a way to track who works for whom, who is in their network, and what content they are sharing. Connections are still made through LinkedIn to be sure, but the attraction is the broadening network of potential contacts and less about the facilitated introduction. People in business search LinkedIn. If you are in business and you aren't on LinkedIn, you don't exist.

Unfortunately, with widespread adoption of social media comes the inevitable and over-whelming amount of noise to sift through. Much of social media today populates the extremes from the mundane (do we really care what your dinner looks like?) to the outrageous and angry. Millions use their social media accounts as a platform to vent their political, religious, and social frustra-tions. It's a legitimate outlet for strong beliefs to be sure, but a baffling one for people in business.

Don't you realize that your customers and prospects are checking out your social media? According to any legitimate measure, half the population believes something different than you do—maybe more than half! Can you really afford to anger and repel half of your prospective cus-tomers? If you are in business, you are crazy if you are ranting about politics or religion online. I have political beliefs, to be sure, I just don't vent them on social media! My kids need to eat and my mort-gage needs to be paid. I'm not trying to restrict your ability to share your beliefs; I'm just ques-tioning your judgment if you do it online.

Think of all the money, time, and effort you spend promoting your business. Every prospect is a golden opportunity, a fragile potential customer relationship needing to be nurtured, encouraged, and converted. Let's say they accept your social media invitation and come to check you out for the first time. Instead of saying "Welcome, how can I serve you?" you question their intelligence, insult their religion, political leader, or viewpoint. When you consistently vent online, you are doing just that. That's just bad business.

Whether online or in person, your tactics need to focus on proximity and relevance, but the strategy has to be to engage in meaningful interaction, hold attention, and be memorable *for the right reasons!*

There are a myriad of tactics that can be employed to raise your visibility, create familiarity, provide engagement, and elicit buy-in from prospects. Quite honestly, each one could comprise an entire chapter, but I am not going to go that deep. For those that apply to your business or venture, I would encourage deeper research on your own. Here is a brief overview of some high engagement marketing tactics with some of the upsides and downsides for each:

Special Events

From bringing prospects, stakeholders, donors, partners, and more onsite, to creating a newsworthy event to draw attention beyond the confines of the event itself, special events have long been a staple of a strong marketing and PR effort. The challenge is that everyone does them and few are newsworthy or noteworthy beyond the stakeholders and their supporters. The key (and a challenging one) is to make your event and cause relevant or attractive to others beyond your core of true believers.

The Children's Tumor Foundation helps provide research and services to children diagnosed with a disfiguring condition called Neurofibromatosis (NF). You would likely never hear about this affliction unless your child or other loved one suffers from it. But you are certain to hear about their annual "Undie-Run." Held around Valentine's Day in dozens of cities all across America, throngs (not thongs) of people run through the streets of major metropolitan cities for about a mile or so and party at a local bar or restaurant before and afterward—in their underwear.

It's a sight to behold as the pink tutus, long johns, gladiator outfits, colorful boxers, skimpy nighties, and a few boring briefs come out in force. The largely tasteful, but always fun run and parties, features people in creative skivvies and with a full range of body types on display for a party that lasts for hours—in the dead of winter. People cheer along the route, take pictures, and generally stare at the unexpected spectacle. It's a great visual that gets widespread television airtime and news coverage because it is interesting and unexpected. The unconventional event also gives the advocates for this cause a wonderful venue to educate and advocate for kids afflicted with NF. (It's a great cause and has brilliant marketing! Check them out at *www.ctf.org*.)

Contests

Historically, contests were developed to capture personal contact information on prospects for future follow up, or to get them to come onsite in hopes of winning a prize. Today, they are used for many of the same reasons, but some very creative companies are taking them to an entirely new level.

Smart companies are now using social media to elicit ideas, feedback, and even content from their customers and fans. The catch-all term for today's contests and surveys is "crowdsourcing."

For example, Doritos encouraged budding filmmakers to create 30-second television commercials featuring their product. What they got was a slew of very creative ads from some talented young filmmakers. The cost for Super Bowl spots is enormous and the risks are equally as large. By taking a chance with young filmmakers, they actually got far more creative ideas than they would have gotten from a traditional ad agency. They chose the best, created additional interest because of the contest, and got props for supporting young filmmakers.

Leveraging this great new user-generated content, they got millions of hits on YouTube, generating buzz from both the idea and the content. Doritos got great commercials to run during the Super Bowl and beyond without any hard production costs.

Others use contests to encourage participation and connection. "Submit a selfie with X product and be entered to win!" Facilitators of group strategic sessions learned a long time ago that when individuals feel a part of the process, they are more invested in the outcome.

Zoos and aquariums across the world have tapped into that dynamic by involving the public in their "Name the Baby Animal" efforts. The news media is complicit in the process as they will show "Ahhhh"-inducing adorable video and pictures of the little critter as people submit thousands of name ideas. Of course, it all gets narrowed down to a few finalists as the public is, once again, asked for their opinion. When the name is announced, that event is covered again. Through the subsequent months or years, people come to visit the zoo to see how that baby has grown. Follow-up stories track the progress and the connection is bolstered.

The top-rated *Today* show in America did the same thing with a cute little yellow Labrador retriever who was being trained as a service dog. The naming contest elicited tens of thousands of votes, with the name "Wrangler" coming out on top. We watched Wrangler grow during the weeks and months. For tens of thousands of viewers, they know that they helped to name the dog!

Lay's potato chips came out with a number of new flavors based on submissions from customers. And though flavors like Chicken & Waffles, Bacon Mac & Cheese, and Cappuccino might not have made it into the regular lineup, it sure made you talk and think about Lay's potato chips!

In your business, what could you crowdsource to encourage engagement? I submitted my last book cover ideas to all my social media followers to get their input on what they liked the best. Of course, in doing so, I was also able to let them know that I had a new book coming out.

You show me an expert who will tell you what the future of social media will look like and I'll show you a liar. The only bankable prediction is the rise of the category itself. The prevalence and importance of social media will no doubt grow; however, the specific forms and companies curating the media are hard to predict.

YouTube

The one consensus is that, for the foreseeable future, video will rule the day. As of this writing, YouTube trails only Google as the top search engine in the world. How are you using video to promote your message, your company, products, people, accomplishments, value, location, attributes, expertise, talents, effectiveness, creativity, and more?

The benefits of video are vast. No longer are you relegated to merely explaining to prospects through ads or brochures what you offer, you can now actually show them. Clearly, television commercials and PR-driven news coverage has long been an option for those with the money to buy spots or hire external agencies. For many small businesses today, YouTube, Vimeo, Periscope, Facebook Video, and others open up a world of opportunities to showcase their wares and build a global legion of fans.

The good news for you (and the bad news for the video production industry) is that you already have a high definition video camera built into your smartphone! Too many have held off on creating promotional videos fearing high production costs. Sure, you can always spring for a professional crew, and the final product can look amazing and be very effective. I hire professionals to edit together my formal preview videos promoting my speaking business. But for most uses, the fact is that you can do it yourself.

The marketplace not only tolerates, but often celebrates reasonable quality video. Hold it in your hand, use a "selfie-stick," or prop it up with a small tripod and you have the ability to tell your own story—in high-def!

Provide a walking tour of your facility or location. Explain your myriad of products. Do a song parody with your team. Offer words of wisdom, inspiration, or explanation. Record yourself or a member of your team demonstrating how to use your product. Provide a review or testimonial. The possibilities are vast.

Be clear, however, like all social media, mere presence on YouTube, Vimeo, or other outlets does not guarantee you anything. The best companies and marketers offer something worthy of being talked about; not just expertise, but engagement. Am I going to learn something I did not know? Am I going to laugh, cry, think, or do something different as a result? Am I going to be entertained and grab friends or colleagues and say "You've got to see this!"?

Of course, the vast majority of video content uploaded every day is entirely dismissible. You know all the garbage that you have to sift through to find something interesting. By the way, it's going to get worse. If you see something good, it was likely passed to you by a friend or colleague, or it was included in an online post or article directing you to a great viral video.

So, why do videos go viral? They do so because they are good, interesting, funny, thought-provoking, shocking, mind-blowing, and different. And even those qualities don't guarantee eyes and ears, they just increase the odds.

Sima Dahl says that before you post something on social media, you need to ask yourself: "Is this post more likely to be forwarded or deleted?" That's a tough standard to live up to. I'm not sure I could pass that test on a consistent basis, but I certainly try to.

Just a few years ago, the differentiator in online presence was simply that—online presence. You had to be there or you couldn't be found and were left out of opportunities. Today, in the world of visibility marketing, everyone is online. In fact, today you are more conspicuous in your absence. You have to be more than merely online or even attractive online. A strong online effort requires being interesting, effective, easy to navigate, clear, creative, strategic, and "buzzworthy."

In the business world, most video content is merely descriptive, educational, or instructive. Make no mistake, I am a big fan of available video content to extend your reach and hours of availability, but video for the sake of video misses the point.

Look at what gets the views: It's the hilarious clips from the late night shows and reality TV singing contestants. It's bloopers and people falling on their face and other "fails." But it's also poignant stories of people overcoming odds and touching military reunions. Then again, zit-popping videos get 100 times the views as new product launches and video rants. The theme once again is: be interesting!

One of the best uses of video is to provide what you would offer if you were face to face with your prospect. You have only to search "How do I" on YouTube and you will find an endless stream of step-by-step instructions on how to install a glass tile, change a tire, potty train your toddler, install a ceiling fan, and more. With this approach, you are establishing your expertise and establishing yourself as the trusted teacher.

Smart companies use video to break down complex processes into easy-to-understand steps. Manuals have become step-by-step demonstrations, and in-person training has given way to live-streaming sessions and on-demand refreshers.

Some of the most popular and effective uses of video content for sales, training, or promotion are "explainer videos." These short, animated videos are used to bolster prospects' understanding of complex business offerings, or to offer a visual illustration of an expert's viewpoint of audio content. The "whiteboard" animations have been around for a while and seemed to have lost their luster a bit, but some are very well produced and have achieved widespread viewership. (The explainer from RSAnimate featuring Daniel Pink's *Drive: The Surprising Truth About What Motivates Us* is a personal favorite.)

Many of the very simple whiteboard animations showing an artist's hand speed-drawing with black marker on a white board have given way to surprisingly affordable, animated, and full color versions that can evoke a myriad of animated styles, color schemes, and genres. Our firm commissioned the creation of animated explainer videos to help business owners and organizational leaders understand the structure and promise of my international team of certified "Visibility Coaches." You can see examples of animated explainer videos targeting small business owners at *www.TheVisibilityCoach.com*.

Not only can these videos be very effective in helping prospects understand your value proposition, they can be viewed again and again on a variety of devices anywhere in the world. Once again, this is visibility marketing. Explainer videos can act as your salesperson or prospector, at least in terms of initial contact. Although the interactivity is missing, you do control the message, the creativity, the delivery vehicle, and promotion.

Keep in mind that none of these tactics in and of themselves are intended to be the magic bullet in your marketing efforts, but can be a valuable weapon in your arsenal as you increase your visibility.

Your Website

Gone are the days where consultants and fellow business owners tout the importance of the website. We already know that. We are now moving into the realm of refreshing, reimagining, upgrading, simplifying, clarifying, and optimizing the website.

Why are companies scrapping $100,000 websites with all the bells and whistles in favor of simple, easy-to-navigate $3,000 (or cheaper) websites? Because they work better and can often lead to the singular behavior that is predictive of actual sales. The mindset is shifting from robust websites that do everything and offer everything, to simple and persuasive websites that get prospects to click, call, or visit. In the end, isn't that what we really want from prospects?

To be clear, if you have an entirely online proposition, with little to no customer conversation, then this cheap, simple strategy doesn't really apply to you. If your business enterprise is an online retail portal, then robustness is the name of the game, although simplification is still the trend. You are playing the price and convenience game, and you might be doing it well, but many, if not most, won't survive it. For the rest of us, the value proposition and competitive advantages you offer through your online storefront must be clear and present within seconds of the first click.

People are busy and impatient and have become used to finding what they want quickly!

And although others have been saying this for a decade, recent online advancements have taken our expectation of quick answers to an absurd new level. We have gone from yesteryear's "Go to the library to research it" and "Look it up in the encyclopedia" to the more recent "Google it on the computer and your smartphone." Today, it's "Siri, when was the last time a dental hygienist placed in the top 50 finishers in the New York Marathon while combating wind speeds over 20 miles per hour?" And we expect an answer!

Visibility marketing is not only about being visible where they are, but being better at anticipating their questions about what they want when they pull their phone out of their pocket or purse. What questions are your prospects asking when they are searching for the solutions that you provide? Can you anticipate them and answer them instantaneously? Recognize that the questions are rarely complex; often they are nothing more than "Where can I find . . . ?" "Who offers . . . ?" "What's the best . . . ?" and so on.

Are you ranked high enough to show up first or near the top, so they look to you for those answers? The first question for you is are you "findable"? And then: is it clear, quickly, that you have what they are looking for? The hard truth is that others do have what they want, and if your prospects can find it quickly from them, you may never have the chance to even compete for their business.

The other issue your customers face is the complexity of your site. If prospects have to read through long paragraphs of text to understand what you do, they won't. If they have to navigate multiple dropdown menus to find what they want, they won't. If they have to decipher your very clever, pithy slogans, taglines, and made up terms to figure out what you actually do, they won't. Are there some who will? Of course. But pointing that out is just an excuse to keep doing what you're doing. The longer you wait to upgrade, simplify, and improve your online experience, the more your competitors get a leg up and the more you will struggle to catch up.

Admittedly, these assertions are contrary to much of what you've been taught through the years about filling your website with robust content, providing deep explanations about who you are and why you do what you do, and giving links to everything that a prospect might want to find, learn, and know about your business so they don't need to look elsewhere. Those rules no longer apply.

Prospective customers no longer have the patience to dig through your jam-packed website. In fact, when they see an overly content-rich website, they click away. Instead of engaging your prospects, you have repelled and frustrated them.

"Do they think I have all day to sift through all this crap?" they think to themselves.

To you, it may not be crap at all. It's your livelihood. You have spent a great deal of time and hard dollars to craft this website with everything customers might need to know and learn about you. We think to ourselves: "If they truly understand how good we are and all that we can do for them, they will want to do business with us." It no longer works that way.

How many of us pick a book that's twice as thick as an average business book or novel and think, "I can't wait to dig into this!"? Some do, to be sure. But most of us think: "Ugh! Who has time to read this?"

It's worse with your website and promotional materials because we are not looking forward to snuggling up with a soft blanket and a warm cup of tea to read your marketing materials. No, we want to find what we want—quickly.

Today, robust, content-rich, and endless page websites are the online version of voice mail hell.

Voice mail version:

"We are experiencing a high volume of calls. Your call is very important to us." (No, it isn't or you would have answered it.)

Website version:

"Hmmmm, how do I find your downtown location and the contact information for a real person? Click here, scroll down the dropdown menu, click second from the bottom, look at the top right hand of that page for the hyperlink; no, not that one, go back to the menu bar, hover over the button, quickly click before it goes away, look for the sitemap . . . grrrrrrrr . . ."

Dump your current website. Go simple, clean, and attractive. What is the most visited website in the world each day? It's Google.com. Go look at their homepage. There is more behind the scenes to be sure, but their value proposition is clear, clean, and right there on the homepage. You may think your website is already clear, with an easy path to find what customers want *because you created it and have been through it a hundred times!* You may also be well-versed in navigating your automated phone attendant. Either way, your customers hate it.

Your website doesn't need to do everything anymore. It just needs to do enough, explain enough, demonstrate enough, and communicate enough to get your prospects to click, call, buy right there, or come visit. Everything else you pack it with isn't just wasted time and energy; it's actually hurting you by repelling prospects who feel overwhelmed and impatient.

Website Design

What do your competitors' websites look like? Does yours look better?

Here is something that might surprise you: did you know that it doesn't cost any more to have a well designed website than it does to have one that looks cheap and amateurish? You don't believe me? Measure your screen. It's a simple space, longer than it is tall, and backlit with a set resolution. What you decide to put in that space is entirely up to you. You decide who to hire and you decide what you will accept and are willing to pay for.

As of this writing, there are over one billion websites with over 12 billion web pages. There are hundreds of thousands of individuals who design websites. Admittedly, some are teenagers working in their parents' basements; whereas others are multinational web development firms offering a wide array of online services. At the end of the day, it'll be one hired designer that is proposing the look and feel for your page.

Rarely are Web designs completely fresh, as they are building on past experiences and success. They are offering you their idea of the best way to present your business online. It's either great or it's not. It's not an issue of money. There are affordable designers and expensive ones. It's their idea and your acceptance. The question is: "How demanding are you?"

This is where I will likely anger many of my talented local colleagues, but the truth is that there are phenomenally talented designers all around the world. Some charge a lot; some charge a little. Some are very talented, whereas others are barely competent. I have paid $300 for stunningly attractive and effective client websites and I have contracted others for tens of thousands and received very poor or marginal work in return.

And though there is some correlation between level of talent and the amount they can get away with charging, I have seen phenomenal talent at very reasonable prices. There is a world of talent available through 99designs.com, Upwork .com (formerly Elance.com), and others. You can go local or you can work with colleagues overseas. It doesn't really matter. What does matter is the work you are willing to accept before you release funds.

The best way to gauge talent and avoid being underserved is to do your research. Look at their past work. More importantly, look at their past ratings and what clients say about working with them. As we, like our clients, are looking to avoid making a bad decision, we have to vet our vendors before we turn over the reins of our brand.

For too many today, the business website is simply a money and time-sucker, frustrating for their customers, and a backlit version of their brochure. For you, it can be a competitive weapon strategically designed to get your prospective customers to stop their search and truly engage with you.

Social Media

Whether you call them your tribe, followers, supporters, minions, or customers, one of the most efficient ways to stay connected with them is through social media. This direct connection mechanism allows for instantaneous messaging, real-time sharing of information, and a deeper level of engagement. The real question is what are you communicating?

Here's the hard truth: 95 percent of businesses simply blow it when it comes to using social media to build their business. Oh, you are likely on social media, but I am pretty sure you can't actually point to real dollars driven from your social media presence and posting. And for the few that can, it often doesn't even cover the costs paid to the social media firm or staffer to run the effort.

So, why then does everyone tout social media as the be-all, end-all, and most important tool in your marketing arsenal? Why isn't it working for you? The truth is that it can be a phenomenal tool if used correctly. The problem is that you are likely treating your social media in the same way as your traditional marketing efforts: talking about yourself, promoting your products, and informing about sales, deals, and specials.

When you treat your social media as just another vehicle to push your advertisements, you teach your audience to ignore you and lose potential fans. You've squandered a golden opportunity to engage them. Instead, you have done the exact opposite—you've made yourself dismissible.

What is the answer then? Don't sell over social media, but rather, share! It's a different mindset. Don't market to your followers, communicate with them. Share wisdom, videos, questions, stories,

quizzes, (appropriate) humor, profound or provocative insight, and success. Reminisce with them
and ask them to "remember when . . . ?" A real
measure of your successful social media efforts is
the amount of people who "like" your post, share
your tweet, comment on your content, and sub-
scribe to your blog or channel.

However, simply getting them to "like" for the
purpose of winning a prize offers a false measure
of success. As 99.999 percent will not win the prize,
most will be disappointed. "Likes" in and of themselves don't paint a very good picture, but it's a way
of saying: "I saw your post. It resonated with me
and I want to go on record as approving or iden-
tifying with it." That's visibility and engagement.

Twitter

Oh, the power of brevity. Successful politicians
perfect the art of the sound bite. Much maligned
as lacking in substance, it's simply an acknowledgment of the realities of how the news media
works. Newspaper and online reporters are looking for quotes. Television producers are looking for
concise comments that work within the confines of
a news story. The soundbite satisfied both. Smart
social media users also master the art as well.

Concise comments, thought-provoking quotes, and meaningful commentary are easy to read and easy to share. Restricting it to 140 characters keeps people accountable.

However, just because content is short and shareable does not mean that it qualifies as interesting, meaningful, or worthy of being passed along. To the contrary, the vast majority of content posted is just noise.

The best (or worst) way to merely blend in with everyone is to spend your days and nights sending "wisdom" and "motivation" written by others. It is staggering how many try to appear wise or inspiring by merely finding pithy quotes that were thought of by others and then sending them out in an effort to be seen as the source for such wisdom. It's akin to building a career in show business by impersonating a famous celebrity. I check my Twitter feed each day and it's like a truck load of business fortune cookies are throwing up on my iPhone. Most of it is simply not creative, not inspiring, and certainly not original.

Just as is true with virtually all strategies and tactics discussed in this book, if you want people to be interested in your Twitter feed, you need to be interesting! Share *your* wisdom, insights, opinions, and content. Engage your audience with content that reinforces *your* expertise, offerings, and solutions. You can (and should) retweet great content, because it establishes you as a resource for information. Just don't confuse passing along articles with trying to connect others' pithy quotes with your brand.

Building up your audience on Twitter can be very valuable as it creates a direct path to share your content. The challenge, like most others in business, is that thousands or tens of thousands are there as well. It's not just about being there, it's about being more interesting there, more repeatable, engaging, and consistent.

The elephant in the room is the subject of outsourcing or automating of tweets and other postings. The reality is that time is precious and I am a big advocate of partnering with others who have time, expertise, and resources that I do not. However, never outsource control of your brand, reputation, and content. Never!

As I am often on stage or on an airplane, others are sometimes charged with sending out my wisdom or posting my blogs; but be clear—they are *my* words and *my* content. Anything with my name on it was written by me. Others will help me build networks, infrastructure, and foster strategy, but I never let anyone put words in my mouth, attach my name to their words, or pretend to be me. Social media requires authenticity with a clear strategy. Others can help you, but only you are you. Never relinquish connection to your content.

Facebook

Once the preferred playground of teens and tweens, Millennials have fled Facebook for "cooler" social media playgrounds like SnapChat, Vine, and Instagram. Good! That leaves Facebook for the rest of us. Few online venues offer the engagement, entertainment, communication, interactivity, and targeted prospecting opportunities that Facebook does. Let the kids roll their eyes at how "uncool" Facebook is. We can do a better job with it than they did anyway!

Facebook is unique and attractive for several reasons:

1. As of this writing, there are over 1.6 billion active users on Facebook. It is essentially the biggest country in the world and you don't need to get on a plane, grab your passport, or clear customs to visit. Everyone is there, so if you are not, you are missing a huge opportunity.

2. You control the content. Don't believe anyone who tries to tell you that your social media should be an open forum. That's crazy! It's your brand, your approach, content, and message. Encourage open discussion and sharing, but delete (or restrict) any content that does not serve your objectives.

3. It's fun! Okay, I'm not suggesting that you slack off from work to have fun. The reality is that engagement is high on Facebook because, for many, it is fun. People like to see who is doing what. The key is to give friends and followers something to read, see, and follow. Once again, business is like high school. When given the choice, we do business with people we like. Facebook gives you a chance to help people know you and like you.

Here is an important reminder about your social media business strategy: Don't "go to the well" too often. It's okay to post about your business, highlighting your promotions, events, staff, success, or even special deals—occasionally! If your fans and followers see you plugging your wares too much, then they will simply leave and not come back. But if you engage, entertain, and involve them, they will forgive the occasional self-promotion. It's a delicate balance. I suggest a ratio of 10:1. Create 10 interesting, entertaining, informative, and interactive posts for every blatantly self-promotional one. If you do more than that, they will tune you out.

Some try to mix the two by offering wisdom and then pitching their product. For example: "In business, the customer may not be right, but it's your job to make things right. Buy my book to learn how!" Don't do this! You don't respond well to pitches like this through social media and your customers don't either.

Part of the beauty of social media is that we get to choose who we follow, like, engage, retweet, share with, and respond to. If you violate the unwritten rules of social media, you will be cast aside for those who do. Don't sell; share!

Studies show that Facebook posts that include pictures and video links get far more comments, likes, forwards, and views. Connect words to visuals.

Other options to explore include:

Instagram

Pinterest

Vine

SnapChat

And yes, I know I left a lot of them out. Ask your employees what they use. Ask your customers and your teenagers. Watch tutorials on YouTube and follow others to see who does this well.

One of the biggest missteps for businesses delving into social media is that they tend to lose excitement and interest in the effort. Often, there is much fanfare from the outset as the blog is launched, the YouTube channel is created, and the page is designed for the Facebook fan page. Unfortunately, no one is specifically put in charge of the effort, or that person leaves their position with the organization. The postings slow, the original strategy is forgotten, and the effectiveness is lost.

Often, it is an overly ambitious strategy to blame if there is no structure to support it. With so many social media vehicles to choose from, there are only a few that we can really keep up with. There's no point in having a blog if it's rarely updated. If you only tweet once a month, your Twitter account basically says: "Welcome. We have no idea what we're doing." You get the picture.

Of course, beyond the diligence needed to create a consistent, online presence and meaningful engagement is knowing when too much is too much. If you are posting on Facebook over a dozen times a day, we are "unfriending" you. If your sharing is overwhelming us, you are not interesting. You are annoying. You are sending the inadvertent message that you have nothing better to do than to post online all day. And you think we have nothing better to do than read your posts all day.

Remember, the purpose of a strategic social media campaign is to create engagement and connection. Behavior that interferes with that end is hurting you rather than helping you. Too often, you get so enamored with your own thoughts, wisdom, selfies, and other musings, that you start to lose perspective. Oversharing online is a bit like body odor. You sometimes need a trusted friend to let you know when you start to stink.

Exercise: The Master Marketing Calendar

When it comes to marketing strategy and tactics, one of the primary mistakes that most businesses make is they approach the effort haphazardly—chasing fads, knee-jerk reactions about an article asserting what's hot and what isn't, or trying something once and abandoning it because of a lack of response. Smart companies are deliberate about their marketing, targeted and intentional in their approach, and plan months in advance.

Find or purchase a large calendar covering the next 12 months. The other option is to print off each month on a piece of paper and spread them out on a conference table, or tack them all to the wall. Make sure each page is big enough to write on. Using a multicolored package of markers and pens, create a "key" or "legend" assigning a different tactic to each color.

For example: Blue=Facebook; Red=Blog posting; Yellow=Magazine articles.

Working with your team, start with the most obvious events and seasonal connections and begin to mark on the calendar those dates or months that might be important times to promote yourself. For example, if you sell gift items primarily to men, you might highlight Father's Day, graduation, and summer months.

If you are working on bolstering your content marketing, you might put a mark every two weeks as a goal for blog posts. If you are writing articles, mark the months that you would like those articles to appear. If you aspire to tweet daily, then there will be a thin line of that color that will run along the top or bottom of those days throughout the entire year. If you have seasonal sales, put the color-coded marks on the calendar. If back to school is an opportunity, then put it down.

This should take the better part of an hour to get everything down, and it might look like a mess, but try to keep it as neat and clear as you can.

As you step back, patterns emerge. There are everyday activities, like social media posts. There are seasonal events that might cause a flurry of activity for a time. There might also be newly-recognized events, holiday tie-ins, and dates that you haven't yet taken advantage of.

Now that everything you can think of has been made visible on the calendar, it's time to prioritize. What can reasonably be done with the resources you have? Push yourself. Stretch yourself. It might seem a bit overwhelming. "Nobody can do all of that," you think to yourself. The good news is that you don't have to do it all at once, just the items that are on the dates when they are due. You'll likely find that you can do more than you have been doing and more than you thought you could.

The most important thing to do with the master calendar is to create a realistic timeline and assign duties.

If you want an item to appear in a national magazine, you have to know that they work three to four months out. A December edition of *Woman* magazine, for example, will need content by July or August, go to press in October, and hit the newsstands in November.

If you are holding a special event, the planning can begin a year in advance. For instance, who is booking the venue, designing the promotional flyer, mailing invitations, confirming the catering, and pitching media?

The Master Marketing Calendar is a broad look at all we have going on to promote our business and when it occurs. The strategy for each tactic and assigning of responsibilities and accountability comes next.

Is it a bit complicated and time consuming? Sure! But what's the point of doing great work in your business if you are ineffective in promoting it? The good news for you is that most of your competitors will not go to these lengths. That attention to the process itself gives you a competitive advantage, but the promotion you do must also be well-conceived and thoughtfully executed.

CHAPTER 8

A Little Paranoia Can Be a Good Thing

Despite how nice, talented, competent, attentive, and attractive (at whatever level) your competitors may be, let's be clear about one thing: they are trying to steal your money! They not only want to take your revenue, they are plotting every day for how to deprive you of your ability to feed your kids, pay your employees, make your mortgage payments, and cover your bills. It's not personal, but you should take it personally! Every time they succeed and every sale they make is at your expense; it's a sale you don't make.

One of the greatest threats to long-term leadership in business is complacency. The landscape is littered with successful companies that lost their market share because they failed to stay on the forefront of product or service innovation, persuasive messaging, and relevance.

It's easy to point to well-known brands such as Kodak, Oldsmobile, Circuit City, Builder's Square, Tower Records, Borders, Blockbuster, and others who once made billions, but fell victim to changing times, appetites, technology, and reacted too late to the "moving cheese" in their category. By the same token, there are a slew of examples of companies that recognized opportunities in their changing market, took advantage of weakened or depleted competitors, and found a way to remain on the leading edge of their category.

American car maker Chrysler was reeling from Japanese competitors who were producing better cars for cheaper prices. American automakers worked hard, but had grown complacent as compared to the burgeoning Japanese competitors. The malaise, combined with entrenched processes and union wage pressures, had driven the major automaker to bankruptcy and was on the brink of failure. Lee Iacocca negotiated a controversial bailout from the U.S. government and led a renaissance that not only changed how they designed and produced cars, but the messaging around it.

Iacocca personally went on TV and apologized for the company's complacency and detailed what they had done to turn things around. The new Chrysler K-cars flew out of showrooms and a new era had begun. To further punctuate the success of the effort, with great ceremony, they paid off their loan early.

Today, complacency is the kiss of death in business. Nobody can afford to get too comfortable. You will rarely be privy to what your competitors are planning or the strategies they will employ until they deploy or launch. Be paranoid. Work each day as if there are countless competitors trying to take you down, steal your livelihood, cause you to lose your home, and drive you into bankruptcy—because there are! Again, it's not personal. Everyone is good and that's the threat in the "new normal."

A simple fable sold millions of copies by illustrating the varying responses to changing markets and the analogy of "moving your cheese" was born. At its core, *Who Moved My Cheese?* is a cleverly crafted cautionary tale, but a reactive one at best. In today's rapid-paced, innovation-around-every-corner, entrepreneur-next-door marketplace, competition comes from both the expected and the unexpected. Those that are complacent can quickly be left behind.

You have to keep your eyes, ears, and mind open. Threats to your market share can come from both the predictable as well as the obscure. Disruption has become a buzzword in business as a new breed of entrepreneur seeks not to merely solve age-old problems, but to ask provocative new questions. Instead of looking to modify current solutions, they are looking at entirely new ways to address how problems are solved.

You may be familiar with the adage that suggests that the do-it-yourselfer doesn't "need" a drill. What they need is a hole. A drill is just the best tool to accomplish the task. Along the same lines, the disruptors look at problems to be solved and take a "zero-based" approach to solving it.

Uber didn't set out to improve the taxi or limousine business. They looked for a better way to use an existing infrastructure of cars to take people from point A to point B. Were the current throngs of taxi operators doing anything wrong? Were limo and town car drivers underperforming? This wasn't the case at all. Competition from an unlikely source caught them off guard.

In every revolution there are winners and losers. It could be argued that the public is the winner with often less expensive, at-the-ready driver options available with Uber, Lyft, and others. The losers simply have to figure out how to compete and innovate to survive.

With every transformative innovation, some consumers will be left to lament the loss, but most will merely wax nostalgic, not really wishing to return to the "good old days." Think of the products and companies of yesteryear that waited too long to recognize a shifting market: Kodak, Blockbuster, Mr. Coffee, Oldsmobile, Atari, and Blackberry. Do we really miss the Yellow Pages, VHS tapes, pay phones, travel agents, pagers, fold-up street maps, disposable cameras, floppy discs, and desk calendars?

Things change. It's a new world and to win for the long term, and not merely compete, it's not about keeping up. You have to be the one to "move the cheese"—and keep moving it!

It boggles my mind when I hear people dismiss the importance of continued, aggressive marketing and innovation by boasting that "our reputation speaks for itself." Worse yet is the ludicrous claim: "We're the best kept secret." As if this is something to be proud of or aspire to. It's not. It's lazy!

Now, I'm not suggesting that a reputation is unimportant. Quite the contrary, your reputation is everything. It is your brand. But relying on your reputation to drive future business is naive and dangerous. Your competitors are aggressively seeking market share and if you are complacent and relying on your reputation, then those conversations with new prospects will be happening without your input. Why on earth would you consciously acquiesce?

The landscape is littered with companies who enjoyed early success, but then rested on their laurels for too long before getting a big wake up call. Some recovered, whereas others waited for too long. Following every significant marketplace innovation has come an eventual raising of the bar for the industry. In short, everyone catches up. Everyone gets better.

When the Dodge Caravan launched in 1984, it included a series of much hyped, "mom-friendly" features like cup holders (revolutionary for their time), 3rd row seating, sliding doors, and more. Today, of course, innovations like these are commonplace. To stay on top, all market leaders must continue to look ahead while keeping a clear eye on those nipping at their heels.

Today, competitors can catch up very quickly. Look at how long Apple took to bring the revolutionary iPhone to market and then routinely takes a year between each subsequent iteration.

Meanwhile, Samsung not only replicates the primary features of the iPhone, but transcends them in a fraction of the time.

Exercise: Go Head-To-Head Against Yourself

Gather your team. Imagine that you are a serial entrepreneur and just got funded to start a company that directly competes with your current company. Work with your team to create a mock company, product, or service that would better meet customer needs than yours does. Start from scratch. Create features, benefits, delivery systems, locations, manufacturing, sourcing, staffing, and marketing messages that take advantage of your deficiencies or shortcomings.

If you have a big enough team, divide them up into multiple teams with the same goal: creating a company and products that are better than your current offerings. Set a significant prize for the winners and give them the time and access to the resources necessary to succeed.

As you work together, ask yourself these very pointed questions:

Where are you vulnerable? What are customers not getting from you or anyone? What can you address, enhance, and bolster, and does it make financial sense to do so? What are long-standing customer complaints? What have customers just come to accept or expect from your industry? Can you step back and see your business from the eyes of your prospects, partners, vendors, and competitors? Finally, how would you market the company or product and compete—against yourself?

Here's the hard truth: there are very creative and motivated people asking those very questions and having those conversations right now! They are happening in technology incubators, college classrooms, and your competitors' offices and boardrooms. Ideas are being shared at coffee shops, on blog posts, and international Skype calls. And every day they are being presented and discussed at thousands of industry conferences and conventions. I know because I am there, often on stage presenting some of those ideas and sparking those conversations.

Are you a part of those conversations—both within your company and as part of your industry? Almost every business industry has a national association representing the various factions of suppliers, vendors, partners, and others serving your industry. Are you a member and are you actively involved?

The best way to know what's ahead or around the curve is to become deeply involved in your industry. Read trade journals and attend the annual conference, not just for your industry, but for the industry associations that your customers and clients attend. And don't just go as an exhibitor, but as an attendee. Go to all the breakout sessions to hear what they are struggling with and what they are learning. Serve on committees or the board of directors for your national industry association.

Keeping a finger on the pulse of your industry is essential to better compete and stay on the leading edge of what is to come. Just as important is to better anticipate threats to your industry and market share.

Most industries hold an annual convention where competitors and vendors gather. For some, it is primarily an exhibition convention where participants can walk the trade show floor getting an idea of what is new and available to bolster the business. Many conferences, however, have an educational focus where both partners and competitors gather to learn about changes in the marketplace, threats to the industry, and broader issues surrounding business, marketing, operations, and so on. Go! Dig into your industry. Learn what some are doing well and where others are falling short.

Too often, I've heard business leaders come back to me saying: "I'm not going to run my business based on what my competitors do!" My response is to remind them that they are not competing in a vacuum. Their prospective customers are considering all options and you'd better know what your competition is doing, thinking, building, and offering. Whether you are looking to stay on the forefront, offer a better product, or a differentiating service, you have to take into account the competitive landscape. Customers have choices. They are always asking themselves: "Who should I choose?"

If you make excuses or simply find it hard to justify leaving your business for a few days to attend your industry's conference or convention, you are missing out. You should attend if nothing more than to keep pace with your competitors who are there. Don't get left out of the conversation! The investment in time and dollars to attend can pay big dividends if you have the discipline to implement what you learn.

The point is that you don't know what you don't know. If your competitors are attending conferences, sitting in on industry task force committees, helping to write regulations, exhibiting their wares, listening to expert speakers, and you are not, then you are at risk. If others are doing deep-dive discussions with their team seeking points of weakness, running competitive scenarios, and rethinking their processes and products, and you are not, then you are at risk.

Another great option is to join established CEO roundtable groups like Vistage, Young Presidents' Organization (YPO), and others. There, you will have your assumptions challenged and have a measure of accountability to prevent complacency. Often, we are so close to our business that we struggle to recognize the loss of drive, effective strategy, or a dysfunctional internal dynamic happening right before our eyes. This dysfunction can make us very vulnerable. Honest, no-holds-barred feedback from our peers can help to fill the gaps in our knowledge and perspective.

Yesteryear's formula for success—a focus on quality, people, service, and hard work—is today's slow death march. Once again, it's not that those foundational attributes are not important; it's that your competitors have already mastered them and are now focused on innovation, disruption, efficiency, micro-trends, data mining, and rethinking traditional approaches to everything.

The future will see a predictable demise of good companies, the loss of livelihood of good people, and the disappearance of good products. In every case, they will be replaced by aggressive companies, hyper-creative people, and disruptive products. And despite some very sad employees and family members of the affected companies, the marketplace will not miss them. In fact, other than fodder for a future *Jeopardy!* question, we will hardly remember them.

The question for you is: Which camp will you be in?

This is not to suggest that every industry will suffer a monumental shakeout. Small businesses will always exist. Pizza joints will dot the landscape, coffee will always pour, and accountants will . . . count. But the world is changing quickly. Yesterday's never-considered product or service becomes the can't-live-without staple of tomorrow. How did we live for millennia without hand sanitizers, smartphones, social media, and GPS?

However, this is not about being left behind, but rather about staying hungry. If you're reading this book, it's because you aren't complacent. You are looking to grow, compete, and not merely survive. Just remember that success can be fleeting for those who don't heed the warning to stay hungry, creative, aggressive, and slightly fearful.

Some fads, however, are destined to fade. I'm not sure that there is anything that Crocs could have done to avoid the "fad" label. The odd shoe's rise to "got-to-have" status was as unexpected as the popularity of parachute pants in the 80s. But just like its odd, baggy cousin to the north, the rapid loss of cool factor for Crocs was easy to predict.

For many companies and even industries, redefining themselves is the only way to survive. Tarnished companies and categories are often faced with such a rapidly changing market that the only way to survive is to change their delivery systems, target market, or products. The odds are rarely in their favor. Often, it's a new player who emerges to adopt the new model, rather than an existing player successfully redefining themselves.

Blockbuster saw the writing on the wall and attempted to move their rentals online, but Netflix was already there. Kodak waited too long to embrace digital photography and by the time they made their move, new players had captured their market share. Creating an impression is a lot easier than changing one. Blockbuster meant checking out physical tapes and DVDs in your mind. Netflix meant streaming. Kodak made and developed film. Megapixels were reserved for newer players.

The good news is that diligence can pay off. Smart companies stay hungry, and can remain on the forefront of industry change and growth. Irrelevance isn't inevitable as long as you keep that entrepreneurial spark and keep abreast of industry happenings, changes, trends, and growth. Hey, look! There goes your cheese! Go get it.

CONCLUSION

Now, Go Back to Number One!

In Brian McKnight's monster hit from 1999, "Back at One," he laid out his five-step process to prove his love. Wisely, he recognized that complacency would doom his relationship, admitting (sing along), "If ever I believe my work is done, then I'll start back at one."

The same holds true with your business. Always look at your marketing as if you were approaching the competitive marketplace for the first time. Unless you are constantly re-examining your business, value propositions, products, services, messaging, and competitive landscape, you are vulnerable. Visibility is not an event; it is an ongoing process of introspection, discovery, creation, implementation, evaluation, modification, implementation, discovery, creation, and promotion. (Yes. I know I said "implementation" twice.)

In 1969, Pete Pyhrr was a young accounting manager at Texas Instruments and developed a revolutionary cost-cutting initiative that he labeled "Zero-Based Budgeting." The concept offered a wholesale shift in how companies planned their activities from year to year. The traditional budgeting process had department heads adopt the previous year's budget as a baseline and then would consider what to add or subtract based on planned activities, organizational objectives, and financial constraints.

The newly developed process asked a different question: If you were to build your department and developed a corresponding action plan from scratch, what would it include? Similarly, there is great value in sitting with your team and asking the same questions. If you were to start your company from scratch today, what would you do differently? What have you learned through the years that would drive different decisions today? What is different about the competitive landscape than when you started? Are there deficiencies or vulnerabilities that you need to address?

As the marketplace is constantly changing in response to changing needs, expectations, innovation, demographic shifts, tastes, and, of course, emerging competitors, we need to remain nimble, flexible, and constantly creative. And though you already have most of that in mind, the need to revisit those issues on a more frequent basis is the hallmark of today's marketplace.

In yesteryear, brands were solid, consistent, and could endure for years, if not decades. Smucker's Jam was a staple, Schwinn was the standard in solid bikes for kids, Ajax cleanser was under everyone's kitchen sink, and Kellogg's Frosted Flakes were always *greeaat!* Today, things can get stale quickly. New brands can emerge quickly. Styles change, expectations change, and what is considered "in" or "out" seems to shift with the wind.

Don't just blame the Millennials for their impatience and fickle nature. We are just as guilty. My friend and emerging workforce guru, Eric Chester, says that all of us stand in front of the microwave oven tapping our foot impatiently as if to say, "C'mon already! I haven't got all minute!"

Now, you might look at your business and think that the changes and disruption don't really apply to your category, but I would suggest no one is immune. Pizza has been pizza for generations. Today, you see choices for gluten-free crust, non-dairy cheese, and variations suited to ethnic and immigrant tastes. This is the case even with traditional commodities: eggs now come from chickens fed omega-3, milk has versions for people with lactose intolerance, and fruit is grown organically. You are not immune to change, enhancement, and a bolstered value proposition.

The other intention of this chapter title is to encourage you to look back to the beginning of the book from time to time and leaf through the pages. Re-examine the questions, assertions, and exercises. Check in a couple of times a year and see how you are doing. Pass it on (or buy more copies!) for new hires to ensure that everyone is on the same page and understand how too many others fall back into poor habits and the very dangerous "conventional wisdom."

Remember that "conventional wisdom" relies on conventional thinking (and that is the antithesis of creative exploration), and "rules of thumb" are only good for counting thumbs.

Here's another controversial bit of advice. If you are big enough to afford a marketing firm or advertising agency, fire them every couple of years and make them reapply along with other hungry competitors. When it comes time for the pitch, don't trust them! Challenge them. Ask hard questions and make them defend their proposed strategy. Look at their suggested course, not from a competency or capabilities perspective, but from a competitive advantage and preferability perspective.

In their groundbreaking *Freakonomics*, Steven Levitt and Stephen Dubner asked unconventional questions and came away with some remarkable and mind-shifting answers. And as they described themselves as "rogue economists," you would be well-served to go "rogue" occasionally yourself to look at your business with fresh eyes.

Of course, not every business and industry is a candidate for disruptive thinking, but yours could always benefit from some unconventional questions.

I began this book with a recounting of a casual, but profound, conversation with my son, Spencer. Out of the mouths of babes can come some very honest questions and observations. Play that role and have others do the same for you. Ask hard questions of yourselves from time to time:

"Could a national competitor move in across the street and take my customers?" "If others came to recruit my best employees, would they stay with me?" "If I fell ill, could my team run the business as

I do?" "If my prime market shifted, do I know how I would replace my customers?" "If a situation, out of my control, made people fearful of the safety of my product, service, or location, would I know how to allay their concerns and survive the crisis?"

The point of this Conclusion is not to merely wrap-up and reinforce the lessons, observations, and assertions, but to remind you that your work is never done. Threats come from many places and will continue to rear their head. Your best hedge against them is to continue to do the self-examination, the deep-dive exercises, the risk assessment, the language crafting, and the overall stepping back that allows you to look at your business with fresh eyes.

The good news is that most of your competitors will not do this hard work. Oh, they will work hard to be sure, but *in* their business and not *on* their business. This gives you a competitive advantage.

My hope is that you have written all over this book, dog-eared the pages, and highlighted words of wisdom. I hope it spurs conversation within your company and challenges your perception of what works and what no longer works in marketing your business.

Visibility marketing is not a new discipline, but a new way of looking at a shift that has already occurred. Look at everything you do, have considered doing, and plan to do in the future. Look at the possibilities through the lens of gauging the visibility impact of all you do. Leverage that visibility to build your brand.

Now, get to work!

If you'd like to keep the conversation going, please connect with me on social media. Find me on Twitter @DavidAvrin or just search me on Google, YouTube, Facebook, and LinkedIn.

INDEX

ABOUT THE AUTHOR

Business marketing expert David Avrin, CSP, is a celebrated author, consultant, and popular business speaker. David has presented for enthusiastic audiences across North America and around the world including Singapore, Bangkok, Melbourne, Buenos Aires, London, Johannesburg, Rotterdam, Monte Carlo, Glasgow, Bangalore, Barcelona, and Dubai.

To learn more about bringing David Avrin in to speak to your audience or work with your organization, visit him online at *www.VisibilityInternational.com* or e-mail him at info@visibilitycoach.com.

David is also President of The Visibility Coach, an international business coaching organization connecting small business owners with marketing and sales experts to offer a higher level of business expertise at an affordable price.

Learn more about business coaching at *www.TheVisibilityCoach.com.*

When he is not traveling the globe challenging and entertaining business audiences, he lives the life of a happy suburban dad to his three kids, Sierra, Sydney, and Spencer, in the south Denver suburb of Castle Rock, Colorado.

David Avrin is also the author of *It's Not Who You Know, It's Who Knows You!* (originally published in 2010 by John Wiley & Sons and updated in 2014 by Classified Press) and *The 20 Best and Worst Questions Reporters Ask* (2009, Classified Press).